IFIP Advances in Information and Communication Technology

Editor-in-Chief

A. Joe Turner, Seneca, SC, USA

Editorial Board

IFIP – The International Federation for Information Processing

IFIP was founded in 1960 under the auspices of UNESCO, following the First World Computer Congress held in Paris the previous year. An umbrella organization for societies working in information processing, IFIP's aim is two-fold: to support information processing within its member countries and to encourage technology transfer to developing nations. As its mission statement clearly states,

> *IFIP's mission is to be the leading, truly international, apolitical organization which encourages and assists in the development, exploitation and application of information technology for the bene t of all people.*

IFIP is a non-profitmaking organization, run almost solely by 2500 volunteers. It operates through a number of technical committees, which organize events and publications. IFIP's events range from an international congress to local seminars, but the most important are:

- The IFIP World Computer Congress, held every second year;
- Open conferences;
- Working conferences.

The flagship event is the IFIP World Computer Congress, at which both invited and contributed papers are presented. Contributed papers are rigorously refereed and the rejection rate is high.

As with the Congress, participation in the open conferences is open to all and papers may be invited or submitted. Again, submitted papers are stringently refereed.

The working conferences are structured differently. They are usually run by a working group and attendance is small and by invitation only. Their purpose is to create an atmosphere conducive to innovation and development. Refereeing is less rigorous and papers are subjected to extensive group discussion.

Publications arising from IFIP events vary. The papers presented at the IFIP World Computer Congress and at open conferences are published as conference proceedings, while the results of the working conferences are often published as collections of selected and edited papers.

Any national society whose primary activity is in information may apply to become a full member of IFIP, although full membership is restricted to one society per country. Full members are entitled to vote at the annual General Assembly, National societies preferring a less committed involvement may apply for associate or corresponding membership. Associate members enjoy the same benefits as full members, but without voting rights. Corresponding members are not represented in IFIP bodies. Affiliated membership is open to non-national societies, and individual and honorary membership schemes are also offered.

Elisabeth de Leeuw
Simone Fischer-Hübner   Lothar Fritsch (Eds.)

Policies
and Research
in Identity
Management

Second IFIP WG 11.6 Working Conference, IDMAN 2010
Oslo, Norway, November 18-19, 2010
Proceedings

 Springer

Volume Editors

Elisabeth de Leeuw
Pracanalaan 80, 1060 RC Amsterdam, The Netherlands
E-mail: elisabeth.de.leeuw@xs4all.nl

Simone Fischer-Hübner
Karlstad University, Department of Computer Science
Universitetsgatan 1, 65188 Karlstad, Sweden
E-mail: simone.fischer-huebner@kau.se

Lothar Fritsch
Norsk Regnesentral
Gaustadaléen 23, PO Box 114 Blindern, 0314 Oslo, Norway
E-mail: lothar.fritsch@nr.no

CR Subject Classification (1998): K.6.5, D.4.6, E.3, J.1

ISSN   1868-4238
ISBN-10   3-642-42381-7 Springer Berlin Heidelberg New York
ISBN-13   978-3-642-42381-9 Springer Berlin Heidelberg New York

springer.com

© IFIP International Federation for Information Processing 2010
Softcover re-print of the Hardcover 1st edition 2010

Typesetting: Camera-ready by author, data conversion by Scientific Publishing Services, Chennai, India
Printed on acid-free paper   219/3180

Preface

The world of the twenty-first century is, more than ever, global and impersonal. Criminal and terrorist threats, both physical and on the Internet, increase by the day. The demand for better methods of identification is growing, not only in companies and organizations, but also in the world at large.

Identity management is put under pressure, due to the growing number of frauds who want to hide their true identity. Identity management challenges the information security research community to focus on interdisciplinary and holistic approaches while retaining the benefits of previous research efforts.

As part of this tendency, surveillance and monitoring are more prominently present in society, both in the public and private domain. The original intention being to contribute to security and safety, surveillance and monitoring might, in some cases, have unintended or even contradictory effects. Besides, the omnipresence of surveillance and monitoring systems might be at daggers drawn with public and democratic liberties.

In this context, IFIP (International Federation for Information Processing) Working Group 11.6 on Identity Management organized its second working conference on Policies and Research in Identity Management (IDMAN 2010) in Oslo, Norway, November 18–19, 2010. Papers offering research contributions focusing on identity management in general and surveillance and monitoring in particular were solicited for submission. The submitted papers were in general of high quality. All papers were reviewed by two to five members of the international Program Committee. Nine of the submitted papers, which are published in these proceedings, were finally unanimously accepted for presentation by the Program Committee.

We are very grateful to the Norwegian government for funding this conference. In addition, the EU FP7 project PrimeLife and the Norwegian Petweb II project supported IDMAN 2010.

We also want to thank the invited speakers, the members of the international Program Committee and the external reviewers, who all did an excellent job reviewing the submitted papers, as well as the members of the Organizing Committee.

October 2010

Elisabeth de Leeuw
Simone Fischer-Hübner
Lothar Fritsch

Organization

IFIP IDMAN 2010 was organized by the Norwegian Computing Center (Norsk Regnesentral) in Oslo, Norway in cooperation with the International Federation for Information Processing (IFIP) WG 11.6 - Identity Management. The conference and the proceedings were supported financially by the Research Council of Norway (Norges Forskningsrådet) and the research council's VERDIKT project PETweb II - Privacy respecting identitiy management for e-Norge.

Executive Committee

Conference General Chair	Elisabeth de Leeuw (The Netherlands)
Program Co-chairs	Simone Fischer-Hübner (Karlstad University, Sweden)
	Lothar Fritsch (Norwegian Computing Center, Norway)
Publication Chair	John Borking (Borking Consultancy, The Netherlands)

Program Committee

Referees

Claudio Agostino Ardagna
Katja Boettcher
Bill Caelli
Jan Camenisch
Andre Deuker
Sara Foresti
Lothar Fritsch
Stefanos Gritzalis
Marit Hansen
Alejandro Hevia
Jaap-Henk Hoepman
Gus Hosein
Bart Jacobs
Spyros Kokolakis

Ronald Leenes
Javier Lopez
Ruud van Munster
Jan Muntermann
Martijn Oostdijk
Ebenezer Paintsil
Aljosa Pasic
Kai Rannenberg
Anne Karen Seip
Rama Subramaniam
Pedro Veiga
Jozef Vyskoc
Bjarte M. Østvold

Sponsoring Institutions

The Research Council of Norway
The Norwegian Computing Center (Norsk Regnesentral)

Table of Contents

Policies and Research in Identity Management

Mixing Identities with Ease

Patrik Bichsel and Jan Camenisch*

IBM Research, Switzerland
{pbi,jca}@zurich.ibm.com
http://www.zurich.ibm.com

Abstract. Anonymous credential systems are a key ingredient for a secure and privacy protecting electronic world. In their full-fledged form, they can realize a broad range of requirements of authentication systems. However, these many features result in a complex system that can be difficult to use. In this paper, we aim to make credential systems easier to employ by providing an architecture and high-level specifications for the different components, transactions and features of the identity mixer anonymous credential system. The specifications abstract away the cryptographic details but they are still sufficiently concrete to enable all features. We demonstrate the use of our framework by applying it to an e-cash scenario.

Keywords: Anonymous Credentials, Architecture, Privacy.

1   Introduction

We all increasingly use electronic services in our daily lives. To do so, we have no choice but to provide plenty of personal information for authorization, billing purposes, or as part of the terms and conditions of service providers. Dispersing all these personal information erodes our privacy and puts us at risk of abuse of this information by criminals. Therefore, these services and their authentication mechanisms should be built in a way that minimizes the disclosed personal information. Indeed, over the past decades, the research community has come up with a large number of privacy-enhancing technologies that can be employed to this end.

A key privacy-enhancing technology are anonymous credential systems [19,5, 14]. In their basic form, they allow a user to obtain a credential from an issuing authority, attesting to her attributes such as her birth date or access rights. Later, she can use the credential to selectively reveal a subset of the attested attributes, without revealing *any* other information (*selective disclosure*). In particular, even if she uses the same credential repeatedly, the different uses cannot be linked to each other. It has been proven that anonymous credentials can be used in practice today (even on Java Cards [2]) and publicly available implementations exist (e.g., www.primelife.eu/results/opensource/33-idemix).

* This work has been funded by the European Community's Seventh Framework Programme (FP7/2007-2013) under grant agreement no. 216483.

E. de Leeuw, S. Fischer-Hübner, L. Fritsch (Eds.): IDMAN 2010, IFIP AICT 343, pp. 1–17, 2010.

The literature provides a number of cryptographic building blocks that allow one to expand this basic functionality; in fact, many of them are needed to meet the practical requirements of a modern public key infrastructure. These include:

Property proofs about attributes allow a credential owner to prove properties about her attributes such as that one attribute is larger than another one (even if they are contained in different credentials). This allows an owner to prove, e.g., that her age lies in a certain range [8], or that an attribute is a member of a given set [9].

Usage limitation such as ensuring that an owner can use a credential (i.e., proof ownership of a credential) only a limited number of times (e.g., for e-cash) [11] or a number of times within some context [10, 12] (e.g., twice per hour or once per election). Furthermore, using domain specific pseudonyms enables the implementation of usage restrictions as it makes a user linkable within a given domain.

Revocation of credentials can be implemented using dynamic accumulators [13, 16] or a form of credential revocation lists [3, 6, 21]. This is necessary for instance to withdraw the right associated with the ownership of the credential or after leakage of the master secret of a user.

Revocation of anonymity in case of abuse of (the rights granted by) a credential can be implemented using techniques from [14].

Verifiable encryption of attributes under some third party's public key [17]. This feature constitutes a generalization of anonymity revocation assuming the user's identity is an attribute encrypted for the party in charge of anonymity revocation. It is a means to control the dispersal of attributes using a trusted entity.

These mechanisms can be combined in various ways. Thereby they allow us to build a multitude of privacy-enhancing applications such as anonymous e-cash, petition systems, pseudonymous reputations systems, or anonymous and oblivious access control systems. It is an enormous challenge to find the balance between offering the whole spectrum of functionality and abstracting away from the cryptographic details when implementing an anonymous credential system. Furthermore, when designing the application programming interface we should require no knowledge of cryptography but only familiarity with the concepts that it realizes. However, reducing complexity bears the risk of tailoring the library towards certain application scenarios which we must avoid. In addition, we require our specifications to be extensible and to go along with current standards.

At IBM Research – Zurich, we have implemented most of the protocols and mechanisms described before. This implementation has been growing over the last couple of years and it has been re-designed and re-implemented several times, the current publicly available version is the forth complete iteration. We were fortunate to receive feed back from a considerable number of universities who have used different versions of our code to build various prototypes. Also, our code has been used in the PRIME and PrimeLife projects to build prototypes, which allowed us to test and discuss our implementation. We believe that the current version provides a good compromise between providing access to the features while ensuring the usability for application developers.

This paper describes the architecture and specification languages for all the interactions of our anonymous credential system called *Identity Mixer*. Due to its generality, the architecture and specification languages also apply to other anonymous credential systems supporting (a subset of) the described features including the one by Brands [5]. In addition, our proposal is extensible, i.e., we allow for the specification of low-level features (e.g., commitments, pseudonyms, and verifiable encryption) that can be utilized to implement a high-level functionality (e.g., reputation system). This fosters the usage of the various functionalities described before and simplifies building applications upon them.

We refer to [22] for the complete set of the specification languages for the components of an anonymous credential system. Here we will discuss the most complex ones and depict them in a human readable pseudo code form rather than providing the XML version used by our implementation. We will incorporate our specification language in the next release of *Identity Mixer* (www.primelife.eu/results/opensource/33-idemix), where several examples for each component will be available. We will demonstrate our framework by elaborating the example of building an e-cash scenario.

Related Work. Camenisch and Van Herreweghen [18] describe the basic functions and protocols of an anonymous credential system and define the APIs for them. The system they describe provides only the very basic functionalities (i.e., selective disclosure and anonymity revocation). We provide much more extensive (and less general) specifications at a slightly lower level, i.e., we do not directly specify anonymity revocation but provide the more flexible verifiable encryption primitive that can be used for the same purpose (cf. Section 1).

Bangerter et al. [1] provide a cryptographic framework that allows security researchers to design privacy-protecting systems and protocols. In this work we go further: we describe our (Java) implementation of all the building blocks described by Bangerter et al. and describe the architecture and specification languages that enable the design and realization of privacy-protecting systems based on our *Identity Mixer* library.

There are various approaches to specify cryptographic objects such as credentials or authentication information. We provide a specification that is general enough to allow to incorporate, for example, X.509 certificates. On the other hand our proof specification could be extended to comply with the OASIS SAML standard. Consequently, we align very well with current standards while still extending their current functionality to a full-fledged anonymous credential system.

Finally, Microsoft has recently released the protocol specification for U-Prove [7], the credential scheme by Brands [5]. That document specifies the cryptographic protocol for issuing credentials and proving possession of a credential with selective attribute disclosure. We provide a much more extensive specification as *Identity Mixer* allows for more features compared to U-Prove (cf. Section 5).

Organization of this Paper. In Section 2 we give a high-level description of anonymous credential systems. Next, we describe the architecture in Section 3, which consists of (1) a description of the different components of the *Identity Mixer* (*idemix*) credential system, (2) a detailed analysis of how those components are used in the *idemix* protocols, and (3) the specification language for the components. We give an example showing how we make use of the specifications to realize an e-cash scheme in Section 4. Section 5 provides a comparison to the U-Prove specification finally we provide an outlook on the integration with current authentication technology in Section 6.

2   Overview of an Anonymous Credential System

An anonymous credential system involves the roles of *issuers, recipients, provers* and *verifiers* (or *relying parties*). Parties acting in those roles execute the issuing protocol, where a credential for the recipient is created by the issuer, or the proving protocol, where the owner creates a proof on behalf of the verifier. An entity (e.g., user, company, government) can assume any role during each protocol run. For instance, a company can act as verifier and run the proof protocol with a user before assuming the role of the issuer and running the issuance protocol (possibly with the same user). Finally, an extended credential system requires the role of trusted third parties who performs tasks such as anonymity revocation, credential revocation, or decryption of (verifiably) encrypted attributes. Usually organizations or governments assume the roles the issuer, verifier and trusted party, and natural persons the ones of recipient and prover.

Note, all parties in an anonymous credential system agree on general system parameters that define the bit length of all relevant parameters as well as the groups that will be used. In practice, these parameters can be distributed together with the code and they must be authenticated.

To participate a user needs to choose her *master secret key* based on the group parameters of the system. This secret allows her to derive pseudonyms, which she can use similar to a session identifier, i.e., it allows the communication partner to link the actions of the user. However, the user can create new pseudonyms at her discretion and all pseudonyms are unlinkable unless the user proves that they are based on the same master secret key. Certain scenarios require one user only having one pseudonym with an organization, where we call such pseudonym a domain pseudonym. In addition to being used for pseudonym generation, the master secret will be encoded into every credential. This constitutes a sharing prevention mechanism as sharing one credential implies sharing all credentials of a user.

The setup procedure for issuers and trusted parties consists of generating public key pairs, create a specification of the services they offer and publish the specification as well as the public key. As an example, an issuer publishes the structure(s) of the credential it issues and its public key.

Let us now elaborate on the issuing and the proving protocol. The credential *issuance protocol* is carried out between an issuer and a recipient with the result of the recipient having a credential. The credential consists of a set of attribute values as well as cryptographic information that allows the owner of the credential (i.e., the recipient) to create a *proof of possession* (also called 'proof of ownership' or 'proof'). When encoding the values into a credential, the issuer and recipient agree on which values the issuer learns and which will remain unknown to it, i.e., they agree on a credential structure. In addition, they agree on the values that will be encoded.

The *proving protocol* requires a prover and a verifier to interact, i.e., the owner of one or several credentials acts as prover in the communication with a verifier. Firstly, the entities define (interactively) what statement will be proved about which attribute value. Secondly, the prover compiles a cryptographic proof that complies with the statements negotiated before. Thirdly, the verifier checks if the given proof is compiled correctly. The first step is a very elaborate process that is outside of the scope of this paper. To indicate the complexity remember that a proof can range from merely proving possession of a credential issued by some issuer to proving detailed statements about the individual attributes. Our specification focuses on the language that expresses the results from the negotiation phase as well as the second and third step from before. The difficulties here lie in the fact that a proof may be linked to a pseudonym of the user's choice or it may release a verifiable encryption of some attribute value under a third party's public key. In addition, we need to be able to express statements about attributes that will be proved. Finally, the protocols for proving possession of credentials and issuing credentials may be combined. In particular, before issuing a new credential, the issuer may require the recipient to release certified attribute values, i.e., prove that she holds a credential issued by another party.

3   Architecture and Specifications

In this section we first discuss the components of *idemix*, then we show how the components are used in the protocols, and finally we provide the specification of the objects used in those protocols. In particular, we introduce the specification languages for the information that needs to be passed between participants.

3.1   Components of *idemix*

An extended anonymous credential system consists of many components. We will introduce them starting with the attributes that are contained in credentials. Continuing with the credentials we will finish the discussion with the optional components such as commitments and pseudonyms, which are used to implement extensions.

Attributes. We denote an attribute a_i as the tuple consisting of *name*, *value* and *type*, i.e., $a_i = \{n_i, v_i, t_i\}$. The name must be unique within its scope (e.g., a credential structure or a commitment), which will allow us to refer to the attribute using that name and the scope. The value refers to the content of the attribute, which is encoded as defined by the type. For each type we define a mapping from the content value to a value that can be used in the cryptographic constructions. Currently, *idemix* supports the attribute types *string*, *int*, *date1900s*, and *enum*. Encoding a string to be used in a group $\mathbb{G}$ with generator g can be achieved by use of a collision-resistant hash function $\mathcal{H} : \{0,1\}^* \rightarrow \mathbb{G}$. Integers do not require such mapping unless they are larger than the order of the group used by *idemix*. In such case, the value will be encoded into several attributes. We chose the granularity of the currently implemented date type as a second and set the origin to 1.1.1900. Enumerated attributes are mapped using a distinct prime according to the description in [9].

Credentials. We denote the set of attributes together with the corresponding cryptographic information as credentials. We classify attributes contained in credentials depending on which party knows the value of an attribute. More concretely, the owner of a credential always knows all attribute values but the issuer or the verifier might not be aware of certain values. During the issuance of a credential we distinguish three sets of attributes as the issuer might *know* a value, have a *commitment* of the value, or the value might be completely *hidden* to him. Let us denote the these sets of attributes by A_k, A_c, and A_h, respectively. Note that the user's master secret, as introduced in Section 2, is always contained in A_h.

When creating a proof of possession of credentials, the user has the possibility to reveal only a selected set of attributes. Therefore, we distinguish the *revealed* attributes, which will be learned by the verifier, from the *unrevealed* attributes. We call the two sets of attributes during the proving protocol A_r and $A_{\bar{r}}$. Note, that each attribute can be assigned to either A_r or $A_{\bar{r}}$ independently of all previous protocols and, in particular, independently of the issuing protocol.

Commitments and Representations of Group Elements. With commitments [20] a user can commit to a value v, which we denote as $C = \mathrm{Comm}(v)$. The commitment has a hiding and a binding property, where hiding refers to the recipient not being able to infer information about v given C and binding refers to the committer not being able to convince a recipient that $C = \mathrm{Comm}(v')$ for a $v' \neq v$. Either of the two properties can be information theoretically achieved where the other will hold computationally.

In our context the bases of a commitment are selected from the bases of the group parameters. When we need the more general version of arbitrarily chosen bases, we call the corresponding object a representation. Where the name is chosen because such objects are representations of group elements w.r.t. other group elements. Representations enable the integration of almost arbitrary proof statements, e.g., they are building blocks for building e-cash schemes or (more generally) cloning prevention for credentials.

Pseudonyms and Domain Pseudonyms. We denote randomized commitments to the master secret as pseudonyms. Thus, a pseudonym is similar to a public key in a traditional PKI and can be used to establish a relation with an organization, e.g., in case a user wants an organization to recognize her as a returning user. In contrast to an ordinary public-secret key pair, however, the user can generate an unlimited number of pseudonyms based on the same master secret without the link between those pseudonyms (i.e., the master secret key) becoming apparent.

A domain pseudonym is a special kind of pseudonym in the sense that a user can create exactly one pseudonym w.r.t. one domain. The domain is specified by a verifier, which allows it to enforce usage control for its domain. Note that no two pseudonyms (be it domain or ordinary) are linkable unless a user proves that the underlying master secret key is the same.

3.2 Protocols

The basic building block of *idemix* is the Camenisch-Lysyanskaya (CL) signature scheme [14, 15] which largely determines the protocols. The signature scheme supports blocks of messages, i.e., with a single signature many messages can be signed. In a simple credential, thus, each attribute value is handled as a separate message. A more elaborate idea is to use a compact encoding as in [9] to combine several attribute values into one message. The signature scheme also supports "blind" signing, where the recipient provides the issuer only with a commitment of the attribute value that will be included in the credential. This is used for attributes of the set A_c. Credentials are always issued to a recipient authenticated with a pseudonym, which ensures that the user's master secret gets "blindly" embedded into the credential.

The distinguishing feature of a CL signature is that it allows a user to prove possession of a signature without revealing the underlying messages or even the signature itself using efficient zero-knowledge proofs of knowledge. Thus, when a prover wants to convince a verifier that she has obtained a credential from an issuer and selectively reveal some of the messages of the credential, she employs a zero-knowledge proof stating that she "knows" a signature by the issuing organization and messages such that signature is valid. As the proof is "zero-knowledge", the user can repeat such a proof as many times as she wants and still it is not possible to link the individual proofs. This statement even holds if the verifier and the issuer pool their information. Of course, a user can also prove possession of several credentials (acquired from different issuers) at once to a verifier and then prove that these credentials share some messages (without revealing the messages).

Let us specify the inputs of the protocols. The issuance protocol requires two inputs for either participant, namely an issuance specification and a set of values. The former is the same for both participants as it defines the issuance process, i.e., it links to the definition of the structure of the credential to be issued or the system parameters. The latter are the values assigned to the attributes of the newly created credential. As we pointed out already, the issuer may operate on a set of the values that differs from the one used by the receiver as A_h are not know to it and for values in A_c the issuer only knows a commitment. Note, the issuer may additionally input cryptographic components into the protocol. This is useful when combining the issuance and the proving protocol, e.g., the issuer can input a commitment received during a previous run of the proving protocol. It can use the value "sealed" in the commitment as the value of an attribute from the set A_c.

The proving protocol most notably makes use of the proof specification, which the prover and the verifier both must provide as input to the protocol. This specification defines all details of the proof. In addition, it links to the necessary elements for compiling and verifying such proof. The prover provides all credentials referenced in the proof specification as input and the verifier uses the credential structures (cf. Section 3.3) to verify the proof. The cryptographic proof object will be provided to the verifier during the protocol run.

Extensions to the Issuing Protocol. The issuing protocol has fewer degrees of freedom compared to the proving protocol. This results from the credential structure setting many limitations on the protocol. For instance, the structure defines which attributes belong to which set (i.e., A_k, A_c, or A_h). Still we provide a mechanism for extending the issuing protocol and use it for implementing a feature that enables efficient updates of the attribute values (A_k) contained in a credential.

Credential Updates. As the issuing protocol is interactive (and for security reasons might need to be executed in a particularly protected environment) re-running it would be impractical in many cases. Rather, *idemix* offers an non-interactive method to update credentials where the issuer publishes update information for credentials such that attribute values are updated if necessary.

This feature can, e.g., be used to implement credential revocation. The mechanism that we have implemented employs epochs for specifying the life time. A credential thus expires and can be re-validated when updating the expiration date (given that the issuer provides such) [13].

Extensions to the Proving Protocol. The proving protocol requires the prover and the verifier to agree on the attribute values that will be revealed during the proof, i.e., all attributes a_i are contained in either A_r or $A_{\bar{r}}$ such that $A_r \cap A_{\bar{r}} = \emptyset$. In addition, the verifier may define what partial information about the attributes $a_i \in A_{\bar{r}}$ has to be proved, where partial information denotes:

Equality. A user can prove equality of attribute values, where the values may be contained in different credentials. In particular, equality proofs can be created among values that are contained in any cryptographic object such as credentials or commitments. As an example, a user can compute a commitment to a value v, with $C = \text{Comm}(v)$. Assuming a value v' is contained in a credential, the user can prove that $v = v'$.

Inequality. Allows a user to prove that an attribute value is larger or smaller than a specified constant or another attribute value.

Set Membership. Each attribute that is contained as a compact encoding as described in [9] enables the user to prove that the attribute value does or does not lie in a given set of values.

Pseudonym. A pseudonym allows a user to establish a linkable connection with a verifier. Furthermore, domain pseudonyms allow a verifier to guarantee that each user only registers one pseudonyms w.r.t. his domain.

Verifiable Encryption. A user can specify an encryption public key under which an attribute value contained in a credential shall be (verifiably) encrypted.

3.3   Specification Languages

As pointed out in Section 1, one challenge when designing the specification languages is to abstract from the underlying cryptography while allowing access to flexible primitives that enable developers to build a broad range of systems. The necessity of both parties having certain information (e.g., the credential structure) in order to extract the semantic of a proof presents another difficulty. For instance, a verifier needs to know the issuer of a credential, the attributes names, their order or their encoding within a credential used in a proof. Thus, it is essential to separate the structural information from the data, where the latter may remain unknown to one communication partner. We will not introduce such separation for objects that do not require it (e.g., public keys). Our specifications are in XML and each component uses and XML schema to define its general structure. Note that the information acquired through unsecured channels needs to be authenticated, which can be attained using a traditional PKI.

System and Group Parameters. The system and group parameters are specified as a list of their elements. In addition, the group parameters contain a link to the system parameters. Both system and group parameters need to be authenticated.

Issuer Key Pair. The issuer key pair consists of a public key and a private key, where mostly the specification of the public key is of interest as the private key as it is never communicated. The public key links to the group parameters with respect to which it has been created. Note that apart from the public key, an issuer needs to publish the structures of the credentials it issues. Even though this information might be included in the public key, we suggest to create a designated file.

Credentials. As mentioned earlier, we decompose credentials into a *credential structure*, which is the public part, and the *credential data*, which is private to the owner of the credential. In addition a credential data object is partially populated and sent to the verifier during the proving protocol. This decomposition is needed in the issuing process, when the credential data has not been created, as well as in the verification protocol, where the verifier does only get to know a selected subset of the credential data.

In Fig. 1 we describe the credential structure. It contains (1) references to the XML schema and the issuer public key and (2) information about the structure of a credential, which is needed to extract the semantics of a proof. We partition the latter into the attribute, feature, and implementation specific information.

```
References{
   Schema = http://www.zurich.ibm.com/security/idemix/credStruct.xsd
   IssuerPublicKey = http:www.ch.ch/passport/ipk/chPassport10.xml
}
Attributes{
   Attribute { FirstName, known, type:string }
   Attribute { LastName, known, type:string }
   Attribute { CivilStatus, known, type:enum }
      { Marriage, Widowed, Divorced  }
   Attribute { Epoch, known, type:int }
}
Features{
   Domain { http://www.ch.ch/passport/v2010 }
   Update  { http://www.ch.ch/passport/v2010/update.xml }
}
Implementation{
   PrimeFactor { CivilStatus:Marriage = 3 }
   PrimeFactor { CivilStatus:Widowed = 7 }
   PrimeFactor { CivilStatus:Divorced = 17 }
   AttributeOrder { FirstName, LastName, CivilStatus, Epoch }
}
```

Fig. 1. Example credential structure where we assume this structure being located at http://www.ch.ch/passport/v2010/chPassport10.xml and corresponding to a Swiss passport. For the XML version refer to [22].

The attribute information defines name, issuance mode (cf. Section 3.1), and type (e.g., string, enumeration) of each attribute. The feature section contains all relevant information about extensions such as domain pseudonyms. Finally, the implementation specific information is mapping general concepts to the actual implementation. As an example, enumerated attributes are implemented using prime encoded attributes [9], which requires the assignment of a distinct prime to each possible attribute value.

The credential data most importantly refers to the credential structure that it is based on. In addition, it contains the (randomized) signature and the values of the attributes. Figure 2 shows a credential created according to the structure provided in Fig. 1 and corresponding to the proof specification given in Fig. 3.

```
References{
   Schema = http://www.zurich.ibm.com/security/idemix/cred.xsd
   Structure = http://www.ch.ch/passport/v2010/chPassport10.xml
}
Elements{
   Signature { A:4923...8422, v:3892...3718, e:8439...9239 }
   Features { Update:http://www.ch.ch/passport/v2010/update/7a3i449.xml }
   Values { FirstName:Patrik; LastName:Bichsel; ... }
}
```

Fig. 2. This example shows a Swiss passport credential. Note that the owner who will act as prover knows all the attribute values.

Credential Updates. Credential update information is twofold: it consists of (1) general information detailing, e.g., which attributes will be updated, and (2) the information specific to each credential. The former is linked from the credential structure (see Fig. 1), the latter is referenced from the credential (see Fig. 2). Only attributes from the set A_k can be updated.

Commitment and Representation. A commitment and a representation, similar to a credential, consist of a set of values. We assume that the bases for the commitments are listed in the same file as the group parameters. Thus, they use a reference to link to the corresponding parameters. The representations, however, list their bases in addition to the list of exponents.

Pseudonym and Domain Pseudonym. As pseudonyms are a special case of commitments, they also contain a reference to the group parameters they make use of. In addition, at the user's side pseudonyms contain the randomization exponent value. Domain pseudonyms additionally link to their domain.

Verifiable Encryption. A verifiable encryption is transferred to a verifier and (if necessary) to the trusted party for decryption. It contains the public key used for the encryption as well as the name used in the proof specification, the label and the ciphertext of the encryption.

Protocol Messages. When running the protocols, there are several messages that are passed between the communication partners. The specification of those objects contains the reference to the schema and the cryptographic values. Each cryptographic value is assigned a name such that the communication partner can retrieve the values easily.

Issuance Specification. Issuing a credential most importantly requires a credential structure and a set of attribute values. As introduced in Section 3.1, the set of values from the issuer may differ from the set of the recipient. More specifically, values of attributes in A_k are known to both recipient and issuer and values of attributes $a_i \in A_h$ are only known to the recipient. For each attribute $a_i \in A_c$ the recipient knows the corresponding value v_i and the issuer only knows a commitment $C = \text{Comm}(v_i)$. We define the issuance modes *known, hidden,* and *committed* in the credential structure to denote the set an attribute belongs to. The reason for defining the issuance mode in the credential structure is to unify the issuance modes between different recipients.

As the majority of the information used in the issuance protocol is defined by the credential structure, the issuance specification is only needed to implement advanced features (e.g., binding a proving and an issuing protocol).

Proof Specification. The proof specification is more elaborate than the issuing specification as the *idemix* anonymous credential system supports many features that require specification. Thus, even when using a specific credential we can imagine a broad range of different proofs to be compiled. We start by specifying an identifier for each distinct value that will be included in a proof. Also, we specify the attribute type of each identifier, where the protocol aborts if the type

```
Declaration{ id1:unrevealed:string; id2:unrevealed:string;
             id3:unrevealed:int; id4:unrevealed:enum;
             id5:revealed:string}
ProvenStatements{
  Credentials{
     randName1:http://www.ch.ch/passport/v2010/chPassport10.xml =
         { FirstName:id1, LastName:id2, CivilStatus:id4 }
     randName2:http://www.ibm.com/employee/employeeCred.xml =
         { LastName:id2, Position:id5, Band:5, YearsOfEmployment:id3 }
  Enums{          randName1:CivilStatus = or[Marriage, Widowed] }
  Inequalities{   {http://www.ibm.com/employee/ipk.xml, geq[id3,4]} }
  Commitments{    randCommName1 = {id1,id2} }
  Representations{ randRepName = {id5,id2; base1,base2} }
  Pseudonyms{      randNymName; http://www.ibm.com/employee/ }
  VerifiableEncryptions{ {PublicKey1, Label, id2} }
  Message { randMsgName = "Term 1:We will use this data only for ..." }
}
```

Fig. 3. Example proof specification using a Swiss passport and an IBM employee credential

of the identifier and the type of an attribute that it identifies do not match. In addition to identifiers, we allow for constants in the proof specification.

We start the definition of the statements to be proved with a list of credentials that the user proves ownership of (i.e., the user proves knowledge of the underlying master secret key). Next, we assign attribute identifiers or constants to the attributes, where the constants will cause an equality proof w.r.t. the constant. Using the same identifier several times creates an equality proof among those attributes (e.g., id2 is used within two credentials). Note that we only need to assign an identifier to attributes that are either revealed or partial information is proved.

Apart from the equality proofs all proofs are specified explicitly. Let us begin with the proofs of set membership for enumerated attributes, where the *idemix* library supports the *and*, *or*, and *not* operators. Those operators can be used on the set of values specified in the credential structure corresponding to the given credential. Similar to set membership proofs, we allow for inequality proofs, i.e., proofs for statements of the form $v_i \circ \hat{v}$, where v_i is an attribute value, $\circ$ is the operator, and $\hat{v}$ can be a constant or another attribute value. Currently, the following operators are implemented: $<$, $>$, $\leq$, and $\geq$. Note that inequality proofs require a reference to group parameters that are to be used, which we provide by linking to an issuer public key.

Relating to the components that we describe in Section 3.1, we specify how commitments, representations, pseudonyms and domain pseudonyms relate to the identifiers. More concretely, the proof specification defines for each exponent of any of those components a corresponding identifier or constant. In addition, all the components of a proof specification are assigned random names, which is mandatory for the identification of the corresponding object in the context of a proof but prevents different proofs from becoming trivially linkable.

4   Example Use Case

In this section we describe how to implement a simple anonymous e-cash scheme with our library to give the reader an idea of how our specifications can be used. We recall the basic idea of anonymous e-cash [4]: The user has an account with the bank under some identity u. To withdraw a coin from the bank, the bank issues the user a credential with the following three attributes ($user_{id}$, $serial_{num}$, $randomizer$) (see Fig. 4). The first one is known to the issuer and is set to U, the other two are not known to the issuer ($serial_{num}$, $randomizer$ $\in A_h$) and are random values chosen from $\mathbb{Z}_q$ by the user as s and r, where q is the order of the groups used for the pseudonyms (and is part of the system parameters). Let g denote the generator of that group (which is part of the group parameters). The form of the credential can be deducted from Fig. 2.

```
References{
    Schema = http://www.zurich.ibm.com/security/idemix/credStruct.xsd
    IssuerPublicKey = http://www.bank.ch/ecash/ipk/credPK.xml
}
Attributes{
    Attribute { UserId, known, type:int }
    Attribute { SerialNum, hidden, type:int }
    Attribute { Randomizer, hidden, type:int }
}
Implementation{
    AttributeOrder { UserId, SerialNum, Randomizer }
}
```

Fig. 4. The credential structure of the e-coin issued by the bank. Let us assume that this structure is located at `http://www.bank.ch/ecash/coin.xml`.

When the user wants to spend a coin anonymously with a merchant, the user obtains from the merchant a random value $v \in \mathbb{Z}_q$, computes $a = u + rv$ (mod q), generates a representation with g^a being the group element, and g and g^v being the bases. Then she generates a proof to show that she owns a credential from the bank where she reveals the attribute $serial_{num}$ and proves that the attributes $user_{id}$ and $randomizer$ are also appearing in the representation. Figure 5 shows the representation object that contains the representation g^a and the bases g and g^v. We provide the proof specification in Fig. 6.

The user then sends (a, s) along with the proof to the merchant who accepts the coin if the proof verifies and if the representation object was indeed computed correctly. The merchant verifies the latter by re-computing the representation. Later, the merchant will deposit the coin with the bank who debits the merchant if the proof verifies. Also, the bank will check whether s has appeared before. If this is the case it will compute u from the two a and v values present in the two deposits (i.e., solve the two linear equations $a_1 = u + rv_1$ (mod q) and $a_2 = u + rv_2$ (mod q) for u) and then punish the user u accordingly (e.g., by charging the user for the extra spending).

```
References{
    Schema = http://www.zurich.ibm.com/security/idemix/rep.xsd
    Params = http://www.zurich.ibm.com/security/idemix/gp.xml
}
Elements{
    Name = ksdfdsel
    Value = 8483...2939
    Bases { 3342...2059, 4953...3049 }
}
```

Fig. 5. This example shows the representation that the user created

```
Declaration{ u1:unrevealed:int; u2:unrevealed:int;
             r1:revealed:int }
ProvenStatements{
    Credentials{
        sfeoilsd:http:www.bank.ch/ecash/coin.xml =
            {UserId:u1, SerialNum:r1, Randomizer:u2};
    Representations{ ksdfdsel = {u1,u2; base1,base2} }
}
```

Fig. 6. The proof specification for the user when spending the e-coin at a merchant. Note that $base1 = g$ and $base2 = g^v$ holds.

5   Comparison with the U-Prove Specification

Microsoft has recently released the specification of the U-Prove protocols by Brands and Paquin. The specification describes the interactive issue protocol between the receiver and the issuer and the mechanisms to present and verify tokens to a verifier. The issue specification defines a number of attributes that will be contained in the token. These attributes are known by both the receiver and the issuer. At the end of the protocol, the receiver possesses a signature by the issuer on the attributes. While they call this signature a U-Prove token we would call it a credential. This issuing process is called a blind signature scheme in the literature, i.e., the issuer does not learn the token that the receiver obtains but only learns the attributes. Brands and Paquin then specify a token presentation algorithm (subset presentation proof). The input to the algorithm is the U-Prove token and the subset of the attributes that shall be disclosed (the other attributes remain hidden to the verifier). The output is an augmented U-Prove token that can then be sent to a verifier who runs the verification procedure to assert the validity of the token w.r.t. to the issuer's public key and the disclosed attributes.

Let us compare the U-Prove specifications to the ones presented in this paper. We do not attempt a cryptographic comparison here. The U-Prove issuing specification realizes a subset of our issuance specification, i.e., U-Prove requires that all attributes have to be known by the issuer, whereas in our specification, some attributes can be hidden from the issuer or only be given by commitments. Thus, it is for instance not possible with U-Prove to issue several credentials (tokens) to the same (pseudonymous) user as this requires all credentials containing a (secret) attribute that is essentially the user's secret key and plays the role of a secret identity.

Similarly to the issuing specification, the proof specification (or token presentation specification) of U-Prove realizes a subset of ours. U-Prove only supports that a subset of the attributes can be disclosed, but does not feature proofs of statements about attributes nor does it provide the possibility to release attributes as commitments or verifiable encryption. Furthermore, U-Prove does not support proving possession of several credentials at the same time and proofs among attributes (be they disclosed or not) contained in different credentials. Furthermore, U-Prove has no support for pseudonyms. Let us finally remark that for cryptographic reasons U-Prove tokens can be presented only once (afterwards the different presentations would become linkable to each other). The *idemix* credentials can be used for an unlimited number of proving protocols without transactions becoming linkable.

Despite the differences in the specifications, it is possible to use U-Prove tokens as part of the framework described in this paper. After all, the U-Prove issuing specification is a means to issue a signature on attributes and it is not hard to extend their specification to cover all the features of our specification. The resulting U-Prove Tokens would still be valid U-Prove Tokens. The same holds for the U-Prove subset presentation proof specification, but of course such extended U-Prove tokens could no longer be verified according to the (unmodified) U-Prove subset presentation proof as the extended proof will necessarily contain new elements.

6   Conclusion

We have provided an architecture and specifications of the components, protocols, and data formats of the *idemix* anonymous credential system. The architecture and specification builds the basis to build a large range of applications that require some form of anonymous authentication. We believe that especially our specification language for the various features of the proving protocol is well-suited for making easy use of the different components such as commitment schemes, verifiable encryption, and representations of group elements. That is, with our specification we enable implementation of systems without having an understanding of the cryptography realizing a feature, in fact, we only require knowledge of the very principle. However, this is the minimal understanding that we can require.

We compared our languages to the U-Prove specification and noticed that the more extensive set of features requires a more powerful language. Our language does not manage to hide all this complexity. Still, we hide all the cryptographic complexity (e.g., which groups need to be used or which exponentiation should be computed) while offering access to primitives that proved helpful when designing various privacy friendly systems.

When it comes to established standards we note that the proof specification together with the corresponding (cryptographic) proof values can be seen as the privacy-enhanced equivalent of an X.509 attribute certificate or SAML token: The proof specification defines the attributes that are stated and the proof values correspond to the digital signature on the certificate/token. We could also integrate with X.509 and SAML by using their formats for the specification of the attribute statement and then derive the proof protocol specification from that. The proof specification and the proof values would in this case be the digital signature. This approach would, however, require some changes in the X.509 and SAML specifications. We leave this as future work.

Acknowledgements

We enjoyed numerous discussions about Identity Mixer and its implementation with far too many people to mention all of them here. Thanks to all of you! We are especially grateful to our collaborators at IBM who contributed in numerous ways: Endre Bangerter, Abhilasha Bhargav-Spantzel, Carl Binding, Anthony Bussani, Thomas Gross, Anna Lysyanskaya, Susan Hohenberger, Els van Herreweghen, Thomas S. Heydt-Benjamin, Phil Janson, Markulf Kohlweiss, Sebastian Mödersheim, Gregory Neven, Franz-Stefan Preiss, abhi shelat, Victor Shoup, Dieter Sommer, Claudio Soriente, Michael Waidner, Andreas Wespi, Greg Zaverucha, and Roger Zimmermann.

References

1. Bangerter, E., Camenisch, J., Lysyanskaya, A.: A cryptographic framework for the controlled release of certified data. In: Christianson, B., Crispo, B., Malcolm, J.A., Roe, M. (eds.) Security Protocols 2004. LNCS, vol. 3957, pp. 20–42. Springer, Heidelberg (2006)
2. Bichsel, P., Camenisch, J., Groß, T., Shoup, V.: Anonymous credentials on a standard Java Card. In: Proc. 16th ACM CCS, pp. 600–610 (November 2009)
3. Boneh, D., Shacham, H.: Group signatures with verifier-local revocation. In: Proc. 11th ACM CCS, pp. 168–177 (2004)
4. Brands, S.: Electronic cash systems based on the representation problem in groups of prime order. In: CRYPTO 1993, pp. 26.1– 26.15 (1993)
5. Brands, S.: Rethinking Public Key Infrastructure and Digital Certificates–Building in Privacy. PhD thesis, Eindhoven Institute of Technology, Eindhoven, The Netherlands (1999)
6. Brands, S., Demuynck, L., Decker, B.D.: A practical system for globally revoking the unlinkable pseudonyms of unknown users. In: Pieprzyk, J., Ghodosi, H., Dawson, E. (eds.) ACISP 2007. LNCS, vol. 4586, pp. 400–415. Springer, Heidelberg (2007)
7. Brands, S., Paquin, C.: U-Prove cryptographic specification v1.0 (March 2010)
8. Camenisch, J., Chaabouni, R., Shelat, A.: Efficient protocols for set membership and range proofs. In: Pieprzyk, J. (ed.) ASIACRYPT 2008. LNCS, vol. 5350, pp. 234–252. Springer, Heidelberg (2008)

9. Camenisch, J., Groß, T.: Efficient attributes for anonymous credentials. In: Proc.15th ACM CCS, pp. 345–356 (November 2008)
10. Camenisch, J., Hohenberger, S., Kohlweiss, M., Lysyanskaya, A., Meyerovich, M.: How to win the clonewars: efficient periodic n-times anonymous authentication. In: Proc. 13th ACM CCS, pp. 201–210 (2006)
11. Camenisch, J., Hohenberger, S., Lysyanskaya, A.: Compact E-cash. In: Cramer, R. (ed.) EUROCRYPT 2005. LNCS, vol. 3494, pp. 302–321. Springer, Heidelberg (2005)
12. Camenisch, J., Hohenberger, S., Lysyanskaya, A.: Balancing accountability and privacy using e-cash (extended abstract). In: De Prisco, R., Yung, M. (eds.) SCN 2006. LNCS, vol. 4116, pp. 141–155. Springer, Heidelberg (2006)
13. Camenisch, J., Kohlweiss, M., Soriente, C.: An accumulator based on bilinear maps and efficient revocation for anonymous credentials. In: Jarecki, S., Tsudik, G. (eds.) Public Key Cryptography – PKC 2009. LNCS, vol. 5443, pp. 481–500. Springer, Heidelberg (2009)
14. Camenisch, J., Lysyanskaya, A.: Efficient non-transferable anonymous multi- show credential system with optional anonymity revocation. In: Pfitzmann, B. (ed.) EUROCRYPT 2001. LNCS, vol. 2045, pp. 93–118. Springer, Heidelberg (2001)
15. Camenisch, J., Lysyanskaya, A.: A signature scheme with efficient protocols. In: Cimato, S., Galdi, C., Persiano, G. (eds.) SCN 2002. LNCS, vol. 2576, pp. 268–289. Springer, Heidelberg (2003)
16. Camenisch, J., Lysyanskaya, A.: Signature schemes and anonymous credentials from bilinear maps. In: Franklin, M. (ed.) CRYPTO 2004. LNCS, vol. 3152, pp. 56–72. Springer, Heidelberg (2004)
17. Camenisch, J., Shoup, V.: Practical verifiable encryption and decryption of discrete logarithms (2002), http://eprint.iacr.org/2002/161
18. Camenisch, J., Van Herreweghen, E.: Design and implementation of the *idemix* anonymous credential system. In: Proc. 9th ACM CCS (2002)
19. Chaum, D.: Untraceable electronic mail, return addresses, and digital pseudonyms. Comm. of the ACM 24(2), 84–88 (1981)
20. Damgård, I.B., Fujisaki, E.: An integer commitment scheme based on groups with hidden order. In: Zheng, Y. (ed.) ASIACRYPT 2002. LNCS, vol. 2501, pp. 125–142. Springer, Heidelberg (2002)
21. Nakanishi, T., Fujii, H., Hira, Y., Funabiki, N.: Revocable group signature schemes with constant costs for signing and verifying. In: Jarecki, S., Tsudik, G. (eds.) PKC 2009. LNCS, vol. 5443, pp. 463–480. Springer, Heidelberg (2009)
22. IBM Research– Zurich, Security Team. Specification of the identity mixer cryptographic library. IBM Research Report RZ 3730, IBM Research Division (April 2010)

Using CardSpace as a Password Manager

Haitham S. Al-Sinani and Chris J. Mitchell

Information Security Group
Royal Holloway, University of London
{H.Al-Sinani,C.Mitchell}@rhul.ac.uk
http://www.isg.rhul.ac.uk

Abstract. In this paper we propose a novel scheme that allows Windows
CardSpace to be used as a password manager, thereby improving the usability and security of password use as well as potentially encouraging
CardSpace adoption. Usernames and passwords are stored in personal
cards, and these cards can be used to sign on transparently to corresponding websites. The scheme does not require any changes to login
servers or to the CardSpace identity selector and, in particular, it does
not require websites to support CardSpace. We describe how the scheme
operates, and give details of a proof-of-concept prototype. Security and
usability analyses are also provided.

1 Introduction

The most common means of user authentication remains the use of passwords,
despite their well-known shortcomings. Moreover, as the number of on-line services requiring passwords continues to grow, users increasingly re-use passwords,
write them down in insecure ways, and/or employ passwords which can be readily guessed. The result is an ever-increasing risk of exposure of passwords to
malicious parties. Users also risk having their passwords stolen [1, 2] through
key logging, phishing, sniffing, shoulder surfing, etc.

A solution that enables the use of site-unique strong passwords whilst main-
taining user security and privacy is thus needed. Password managers of various
types have been proposed to meet this need [3]. A password manager stores usernames and passwords and makes them available when required. Users are not
required to remember any passwords apart from a single master password which
can be used to lock/un-lock the password manager. Password managers can be
particularly helpful when a relatively large number of passwords are required
to access multiple on-line services. Password managers can be seen as potential
alternatives to single sign-on systems such as Windows Live ID, formally known
as Passport (http://passport.net/), and OpenID (http://openid.net/).

Windows CardSpace is a user-friendly tool supporting user authentication.
Instead of providing a username and password, a CardSpace user selects a virtual
card, known as an information card (InfoCard), from an intuitive user interface
provided by the CardSpace identity selector (CIdS), to sign on to a website.

Despite the introduction of CardSpace (and other similar systems), the vast
majority of websites still use username-password for authentication, and this is

E. de Leeuw, S. Fischer-Hübner, L. Fritsch (Eds.): IDMAN 2010, IFIP AICT 343, pp. 18–30, 2010.

likely to continue for at least the next few years [2]. One major problem with CardSpace, and with other similar systems providing more secure means of user authentication, is that the transition from username-password to full-blown identity management is extremely difficult to achieve. Service providers (SPs) will not wish to do the work necessary to support CardSpace if very few users employ it; equally, users are hardly likely to use CardSpace if it is only supported by a small minority of websites. The scheme we describe is designed to help overcome this barrier to change by allowing an evolutionary deployment of CardSpace, initially as a password manager and subsequently, once users are familiar with its interface, as a more sophisticated means of user authentication.

In this paper we propose a simple scheme that uses the CIdS as a password manager. The goal is to develop a simple and intuitive approach to password management, transparent to both the CIdS and SPs. The technique we describe works with existing servers without any modifications, and, in particular, SPs are not required to support CardSpace.

The remainder of the paper is organised as follows. Section 2 presents an overview of CardSpace, and Sect. 3 describes the proposed scheme. We describe a prototype implementation in Sect. 4, and, in Sect. 5, we provide security and usability analyses. Sect. 6 reviews related work and Sect. 7 concludes the paper.

2   CardSpace

This section gives a brief introduction to CardSpace, including a description of the use of CardSpace personal cards.

2.1   Introduction

Microsoft CardSpace is an identity management system that provides a secure and consistent way for users to control and manage personal data, to review personal data before sending it to a website, and to verify the identity of visited websites. It also enables websites to obtain personal information from users, e.g. to support user authentication and authorisation.

The CIdS enables users to manage digital identities issued by a variety of identity providers (IdPs), and use them to access on-line services. Digital identities are visually represented to users as InfoCards, and are implemented as XML files that list the types of claim made by one party about itself or another party.

The concept of an InfoCard is inspired by real-world cards, e.g. credit cards. Users can employ one (virtual) InfoCard to identify themselves to multiple websites. Alternatively, separate InfoCards can be used in distinct situations. Websites can request different types of cards and/or different types of claims.

There are two types of InfoCards: personal (self-issued) cards and managed cards. Personal cards are created by users themselves, and the claims listed in such an InfoCard are asserted by the self-issued identity provider (SIP) that co-exists with the CIdS on the user machine. Managed cards, on the other hand, are obtained from remote IdPs [4–8].

By default, CardSpace is supported in Internet Explorer (IE) from version 7 onwards. Extensions to other browsers, such as Firefox[1] and Safari[2], also exist. Microsoft has recently released an updated version of CardSpace, known as Windows CardSpace 2.0 Beta 2[3]. However, in this paper we refer throughout to the CardSpace version that is shipped by default as part of Windows Vista and Windows 7, which has also been approved as an OASIS standard under the name 'Identity Metasystem Interoperability Version 1.0' (IMI 1.0) [9].

2.2 Personal Cards

The core idea introduced here is to use CardSpace personal cards to enable users to seamlessly authenticate to websites using stored passwords. We therefore first describe how personal cards are used.

Overview. Prerequisites for use of a personal card include a CardSpace-enabled relying party (RP) and a CardSpace-enabled user agent, e.g. a web browser capable of invoking the CIdS. The CIdS enables the creation of personal cards, which currently support 14 editable claim types, namely *First Name, Last Name, Email Address, Street, City, State, Postal Code, Country/Region, Home Phone, Other Phone, Mobile Phone, Date of Birth, Gender*, and *Web Page*.

Using Personal Cards. When using personal cards, CardSpace adopts the following protocol. We assume here that the RP does not employ a security token service (STS)[4].

1. User agent → RP. HTTP/S request: GET (a login page).
2. RP → user agent. HTTP/S response. A login page is returned containing CardSpace-enabling tags in which the RP security policy is embedded.
3. The user agent offers the user the option to use CardSpace (e.g. via a button on the RP web page), and selection of this option causes the agent to invoke the CIdS and pass it the RP policy. Note that if this is the first time that this RP has been contacted, the CIdS will display the RP identity and give the user the option to either proceed or abort the protocol.
4. After evaluating the RP policy, the CIdS highlights the InfoCards matching the policy, and greys out the rest. InfoCards previously used for this particular RP are displayed in the upper half of the selector screen.
5. The user chooses a personal card. (Alternatively, the user could create and choose a new personal card). At this point the user can check the requested claim types and decide whether or not to proceed. Note that the selected InfoCard may contain several claims, but only the claims explicitly requested in the RP security policy will be passed to the requesting RP.

---

[1] https://addons.mozilla.org/en-US/firefox/addon/10292
[2] http://www.hccp.org/safari-plug-in.html
[3] http://technet.microsoft.com/en-us/library/dd996657(WS.10).aspx
[4] An STS is a software component responsible for security policy and token management within an IdP and, optionally, within an RP.

6. The CIdS creates and sends a SAML-based request security token (RST) to the SIP, which responds with a SAML-based request security token response (RSTR).
7. The RSTR is then passed to the user agent, which forwards it to the RP.
8. The RP validates the received SAML token, and, if satisfied, grants access to the user.

Details of how CardSpace managed cards are used are given in the relevant specifications [4–6, 9].

3 A CardSpace-Based Password Manager (CPM)

We next give an overview of the CPM, covering relevant operational aspects.

3.1 Browser Extension

The CPM is based on a browser extension that can read and modify browser-rendered web pages. It can also read CardSpace-issued RSTR tokens. In addition it can automatically fill and submit login forms, start automatically, and be enabled or disabled by the user.

3.2 PassCards

Either prior to, or during, use of the CPM, the user must first create a personal card, referred to here as a PassCard, containing a username and password. Basic protection against phishing is provided if the URL of the target website is included in the PassCard. However, this is optional, as users may wish to use a single PassCard with multiple websites sharing the same user credentials.

The browser extension is responsible for adding the PassCard logo (see Fig. 3), a modified version of the CardSpace logo, to the SP web page, enabling the user to invoke the CIdS and to subsequently select (or create) a PassCard.

3.3 System Parties

The parties involved are as follows.

– An SP, i.e. a website that the user is currently visiting.
– A CardSpace-enabled user agent (e.g. a suitable web browser, such as IE8).
– A browser extension implementing the protocol described below.

3.4 Message Flows

The protocol steps, as shown in Fig. 1, are as follows.

1. User agent → SP. HTTP request: GET (a login page).
2. SP → user agent. HTTP response: (the login page is returned).

3. The browser extension performs the following processes using the login page provided by the SP.
   (a) It scans the page for a login form containing a username and password field and a submit button.
   (b) If all of these are found, it highlights the username and password fields.
   (c) It adds CardSpace-enabling tags to the login page, setting the associated security policy to require a token asserting claims of the types in which the user credentials are stored (see Sect. 3.5 for a discussion of what occurs when interacting with SPs that already support CardSpace.)
   (d) It adds a function to the login page to intercept the RSTR that will later be returned by the CIdS.
   (e) It causes the PassCard logo to appear above the submit button, in such a way that clicking it invokes the CIdS.
4. The user clicks on the PassCard logo and the CIdS lights up. If this is the first time that this SP has been contacted, the CIdS will display the SP identity and give the user the option to either proceed or abort the protocol. On proceeding, the CIdS highlights the InfoCards that match the policy statement added by the browser extension, and greys out the rest. InfoCards previously used for this SP are displayed in the upper half of the selector screen.
5. The user selects and submits a PassCard. Alternatively, the user could create and choose a new PassCard. The CIdS creates and sends a SAML-based RST to the SIP, which responds with a SAML-based RSTR.
6. The CIdS passes the RSTR to the browser.
7. The browser extension performs the following tasks.
   (a) It intercepts and parses the RSTR.
   (b) If the RSTR contains the URL of the target website, it compares it with the URL of the visited website, and only proceeds if they match.
   (c) It extracts the username and password values.
   (d) It auto-populates and auto-submits the login form.
8. The SP verifies the credentials, and, if satisfied, grants access.

Note that the CPM user experience is precisely the same to that of 'conventional' password-based authentication except that, instead of manually entering and submitting a username and password, the CPM user selects and submits a virtual card.

3.5   CardSpace-Enabled SPs

Regardless of whether or not an SP already supports CardSpace, the browser extension will always add the PassCard logo to the SP web page, as long as it detects username-password prompts on the page. This means that, if an SP supports CardSpace and simultaneously supports username-password authentication, as does the 'myOpenID' website (https://www.myopenid.com/ [sampled on 5/1/2010]), the browser extension will still insert the PassCard logo above the submit button of the password-based login form. Informal tests on the prototype

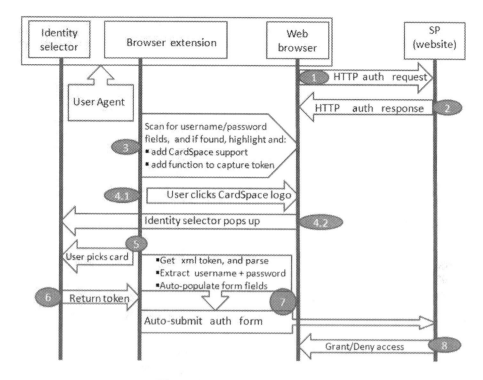

Fig. 1. CPM message exchanges

implementation (see Sect. 4) suggest that this will not disrupt the normal operation of CardSpace; indeed, the browser extension does not modify the original SP-CardSpace-enabling tags in any way.

The SP page will thus display the CardSpace and PassCard logos. In this case, users will have (at least) three login options:

1. populating the username and password fields and submitting the login form manually;
2. using the CPM to automatically populate and submit the login form; or
3. clicking the CardSpace logo to use CardSpace-based authentication.

Note that hovering the mouse over the PassCard logo results in the display of text indicating that clicking it will activate the CPM.

4   Prototype Realisation

We next give details of a prototype implementation of the scheme.

The prototype is coded as a plug-in[5] using JavaScript [10], chosen because its wide adoption should simplify the task of porting the prototype to a range of

---

[5] The term 'plug-in' is used here to refer to any client-side browser extension, such as a user script, plug-in, etc.

other browsers. It uses the Document Object Model (DOM) [11] to inspect and manipulate HTML pages and XML documents. We plan to publish the CPM prototype as an open source research project.

4.1 Registration

Prior to, or during, use of the CPM, the user invokes the CIdS and creates a PassCard, inserting their username in the *firstname* field and password in the *lastname* field. Optionally, the user could also insert the URL of the target website in the *web page* field[6] (see Sect. 3.2). For ease of identification, the user can give the PassCard a meaningful name, e.g. of the corresponding website. The user can also upload an image for the PassCard, e.g. containing the logo of the intended site. Example PassCards are shown in Fig. 2.

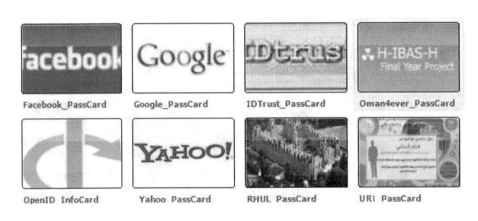

Fig. 2. PassCards

4.2 Implementation

The prototype implements the message exchanges specified in Sect. 3.4; we refer throughout to the step numbers given there.

Prototype-specific Implementation Details. In step 3, the plug-in processes the SP web page in the following way.

1. The plug-in scans the web page for a login form containing a pair of username and password fields and a submit button. More specifically, the following procedure is used.
   (a) The plug-in scans the web page for a form tag.
   (b) If a form tag is found, it searches the form for three input tags referring to username, password, and submit, as follows:

---

[6] The *web page* field was chosen to contain the URL of the target website since it seemed the logical choice; however, this is an implementation option.

i. it searches for an input tag of type 'text';

ii. if found, it searches for another input tag of type 'password'; and

iii. if found, it searches for another input tag of type 'submit'[7].

(c) If all three fields are detected, then the plug-in highlights the username and password fields in green for ease of identification.

The above process involves the following detailed processing.

– Highlighting does not take place unless both the username and password fields and the submit button have been detected in a single form, as a web page could potentially contain more than one input tag of type 'text', such as those used for searching.

– To differentiate between registration and login web pages, the plug-in terminates if it detects more than one password field between the username and submit fields. Whereas it appears common for a login page to only have a single password field before the submit button, registration pages typically have two password fields (before the submit button): the first for the user to enter their password, and the second to confirm their password. Examples include the registration and login pages hosted by major websites, such as Google, YouTube, Yahoo, Microsoft Research, SpringerLink[8], etc.

– When searching for the form submission button, if no submitting input tag has been found the plug-in searches for an 'image' tag. This is because, instead of a submit button, some websites display a clickable image[9] with similar functionality.

– Whereas it appears common for a username field to be immediately followed by a password field, a submit button may not always immediately follow a password field. For example, some major websites (e.g. Google, YouTube, Yahoo, Gmail, SpringerLink) add a 'Stay signed in' or 'Remember me' check box between the password field and the submit button[10]. The plug-in addresses this issue by skipping all tags between the password field and the submit button, including those of type 'checkbox'.

2. The plug-in adds an HTML object tag that allows the user to invoke the CIdS. Within the object tag, the plug-in sets the param tags to indicate that the SP security policy requires PassCards to contain two fields: the *firstname* and the *lastname* fields, (or three fields if protection against phishing is required, in which case the third field would be the *web page* field). Alternatively, the security policy could be configured so that the *web page* field is optional.

3. The plug-in adds a function to the head section of the SP login page to intercept the XML-based RSTR message returned by the CIdS.

---

[7] If no input tag of type 'submit' is found, the plug-in searches for an input tag of type 'image' and, if still not found, it then searches for an event-based input tag of type 'button'.

[8] Websites most recently checked on 5/1/2010.

[9] This includes an image tag embedded in a hyperlink (anchor) tag, an image tag on its own, an image tag embedded inside a button tag, an event-based button tag, etc.

[10] Websites most recently checked on 5/1/2010.

4. The plug-in inserts the PassCard logo in the login web page, causing it to appear just before the 'login' button, as shown in Fig. 3. The logo is associated with an 'on-click' event so that, if clicked, the CIdS is invoked (after calling the added function). To cater for users with sight difficulties or web browsers configured not to display images, a text field can replace the logo. This text is also displayed when the mouse is held over the PassCard logo, indicating that the CPM can be used to sign on.

After step 6, the plug-in performs the following steps.

1. It intercepts the XML-based RSTR using the added function.
2. It parses the intercepted token and extracts the values of the *firstname* and *lastname* fields. The plug-in uses an XML parser built into the browser to read and manipulate the intercepted XML token. The plug-in passes the token to the parser, which reads it and converts it into an XML DOM object that can be accessed and manipulated by JavaScript.
3. If a URL is stored in the PassCard, it compares the stored URL with the URL of the visited website, and only proceeds if they match.
4. It automatically fills in the username and password fields with the *firstname* and *lastname* values, respectively.
5. It auto-submits the login form using the JavaScript 'click()' method.

Fig. 3. PassCard logo

Coding Environment. The JavaScript-driven plug-in was built using IE7PRO, an IE extension, chosen to simplify prototype implementation. Users of the prototype must therefore install IE7PRO, freely available at the IE7PRO website (http://ie7pro.com), prior to installing the CPM plug-in. To enable or disable the prototype, a user can simply tick or un-tick the appropriate entry in the 'IE7PRO Preferences' interface, thus meeting the final objective listed in Sect. 3.1.

An IE7PRO-free version has also been produced. In this latest version, the JavaScript code is executed using a C#-driven browser helper object (BHO), a Dynamic-link library (DLL) module designed as a plug-in for IE that, once installed, attaches itself to IE, thus gaining access to the current page's DOM. The CPM prototype can readily be enabled or disabled using the add-on manager in the IE *Tools* menu.

5   Discussion and Analysis

We now consider a number of CPM features, and also review certain limitations.

5.1   CPM Features

Security. The CPM takes advantage of the CIdS, and is supported by its built-in security features. For example, when invoked, the CIdS runs in a separate private desktop session, preventing other applications, e.g. malware, from interacting or interfering with it. In addition, all values inserted in the fields of a PassCard are stored in encrypted form on the user machine.

Furthermore, in protocol step 4 of the CPM, the CIdS identifies the SP to the user and indicates whether or not they have visited that particular SP before; if the user is visiting this SP for the first time, CardSpace requests the user's permission to proceed[11] (see section 3.4). This helps to support mutual authentication since the user and the SP are both identified to each other.

As with any local password manager, the CPM avoids the need for trusted third parties. In addition, the automatic form-filling feature reduces exposure to shoulder-surfing attacks and also helps to thwart key loggers.

The CPM reduces the threat of phishing attacks involving impersonation of legitimate sites by comparing the URL in the PassCard with that of the visited website. The CPM also supports the use of strong per-site passwords, since users no longer need to memorise or write down passwords.

Finally, the CPM browser extension does not require any changes to default IE security settings, thus avoiding potential vulnerabilities resulting from lowered browser security settings.

Usability. The CPM provides a simple, intuitive user experience through its use of the CIdS interface. At the same time, it familiarises users with CardSpace, thereby potentially facilitating future adoption of more secure means of authentication. Unlike other password managers which represent credentials in text form, CPM credentials are stored in PassCards which can be equipped with a readily recognisable image, e.g. an SP logo.

The CPM operates completely transparently to external parties, and hence does not require any changes to SPs, identity selectors or to default browser security settings. The scheme is also highly flexible, since users can choose whether or not to use it simply by electing to click the PassCard logo (or not).

---

[11] This enhances security by comparison with 'conventional' password-based authentication, where the SP is not identified to the user.

Finally, by making use of CardSpace features, the CPM supports a degree of roaming. A user can transfer PassCards from one PC to another using the CardSpace backup facilities. Indeed, if the CardSpace backup file (which holds data in encrypted form) is stored on a portable storage medium (e.g. a USB drive) then full mobility is provided, as well as robustness in the form of protection against loss of credential data.

5.2   Limitations and Countermeasures

Perhaps the most obvious limitation of the CPM is that anyone with access to a Windows user account can access the PassCards and use the stored credentials. This is a fundamental limitation of CardSpace which, by default, does not impose any additional password protection on the use of the CIdS. To address this issue, we observe that CardSpace allows individual InfoCards to be PIN-protected, which should be seriously considered for PassCards stored on a machine which is not physically secure. In addition, it may be possible to cause CardSpace to run under User Account Control (UAC), so that running CardSpace causes Windows to prompt the user for an admin password.

The version of the CPM prototype described in this paper does not work as intended with websites employing TLS/SSL encryption because, if the SP has a certificate, then the CIdS will, by default, encrypt the SAML-based RSTR message using the public key of the requesting SP. The plug-in does not have access to the SP's private key, and hence will be unable to decrypt the token. As a result, the CPM will not be able to perform automatic form-filling as it cannot obtain the username/password values. However, because the CPM (if clicked) automatically invokes the CIdS, users could manually copy and paste the required credentials from the relevant PassCard into the login form. This is particularly simple if only a password is needed.

A more satisfactory solution to this issue would be to configure the CPM to redirect the user to an (arbitrary) HTTP-based website whenever an HTTPS-based website is visited. In this case, the CPM could read the SAML token returned from the CIdS as it would not be encrypted. The CPM could then submit the credentials automatically to the target HTTPS-based site. The transfer could be achieved using hidden HTML form variables or URL query parameters. We are currently developing a prototype to realise this.

The browser extension must scan every browser-rendered web page to detect whether it supports username-password authentication, and this may affect system performance. However, informal tests on the CPM prototype suggest that this is not a serious issue. In addition, the browser extension can be configured so that it only operates with certain websites.

The current CPM prototype has not yet been tested with the recently released CardSpace 2.0[12]. We are thus unable to provide precise operational details for this version.

---

[12] CardSpace 2.0 has not yet been standardised; in fact, at the time of writing, CardSpace 2.0 has only been released as a *Beta* prototype.

Finally, older browsers (or browsers with scripting disabled) may not be able to run the CPM, as it was built using JavaScript. However, most modern browsers support JavaScript (or ECMAscript), and so this is not a major usability obstacle.

6   Related Work

Password managers, which store passwords in a secure location either on the user PC or remotely, are now widely available. They typically store passwords in encrypted form and, unlike the CPM, require users to use a single master password to access the password store. Some are also capable of masking passwords, and others, much like the CPM, provide automatic password entry. Examples of password managers include open source schemes such as Password Safe (http://passwordsafe.sourceforge.net/), KeePass (http://KeePass.info/), Qubliette (http://tranglos.com/free/oubliette.html), Password Gorilla (http://fpx.de/fp/Software/Gorilla/) and PINs (mirekw.com/winfreeware/pins.html) as well as commercial products such as RoboForm (http://roboform.com/), Any Password (http://anypassword.com/) and Turbopasswords (http://chapura.com/passwordmanager.php).

Perhaps the most distinctive feature of the CPM is its dependence on CardSpace, whereas other password managers are independent applications. As a result, the CPM can benefit significantly from the CardSpace security features. The CPM's use of CardSpace may also give users greater confidence in its security features. Most importantly, it is hoped that the introduction of a scheme like the CPM, with immediate practical benefits to the end user, will help encourage the adoption of more sophisticated identity management systems like CardSpace. Such identity management schemes offer the potential for a step forward in the practice of user authentication and authorisation, with potential benefits for all legitimate parties operating via the Internet. Indeed, without simple paths to adoption for schemes like CardSpace, there is a danger that it and all the other identity initiatives will fail.

7   Conclusions and Future Work

In this paper we have proposed a novel scheme that enables CardSpace to be used as a password manager. Users store their usernames and passwords in CardSpace personal cards, and use such cards to transparently sign on to corresponding websites. The scheme is based on a browser extension, and requires no changes to login servers; in particular, it does not require them to support CardSpace. Neither does the scheme require any changes to the current CIdS.

The scheme uses the CIdS interface to seamlessly authenticate users to websites. It extends the use of personal cards to allow for transparent password management. Such an approach could help to extend the applicability of CardSpace, as well as encouraging its adoption.

Planned future work includes building a portable version of the CPM to support users who do not have installation privileges or are forced to use untrusted machines when travelling. In addition, we plan to investigate the possibility of using CardSpace as a password-based single sign-on system.

Acknowledgements

The first author is sponsored by the Diwan of Royal Court, Sultanate of Oman. The helpful remarks provided by anonymous referees are gratefully acknowledged. Finally, we would like to thank Cormac Herley for his guidance and support.

References

1. Conklin, A., Dietrich, G., Walz, D.: Password-based authentication: a system perspective. In: Proceedings of the 37th Annual Hawaii International Conference on System Sciences (HICSS 04)–Track 7, p. 70170b. IEEE Computer Society, Los Alamitos (2004)
2. Herley, C., van Oorschot, P.C., Patrick, A.S.: Passwords: If we're so smart, why are we still using them? In: Dingledine, R., Golle, P. (eds.) FC 2009. LNCS, vol. 5628, pp. 230–237. Springer, Heidelberg (2009)
3. De Luca, M.: Password Management for Distributed Environments. VDM Verlag, Saarbrücken (2008)
4. Jones, M.B.: A Guide to Using the Identity Selector Interoperability Profile V1.5 within Web Applications and Browsers. Microsoft Corporation (2008)
5. Bertocci, V., Serack, G., Baker, C.: Understanding Windows CardSpace: An Introduction to the Concepts and Challenges of Digital Identities. Addison-Wesley, Reading (2008)
6. Mercuri, M.: Beginning Information Cards and CardSpace: From Novice to Professional. Apress, New York (2007)
7. Oppliger, R., Gajek, S., Hauser, R.: Security of Microsoft's identity metasystem and CardSpace. In: Proceedings of the Kommunikation in Verteilten Systemen (KiVS 2007), pp. 63–74. VDE Publishing House, Berlin (2007)
8. Al-Sinani, H.S., Alrodhan, W.A., Mitchell, C.J.: CardSpace-Liberty integration for CardSpace users. In: Proceedings of the 9th Symposium on Identity and Trust on the Internet (IDtrust 2010), pp. 12–25. ACM, New York (2010)
9. Jones, M.B., McIntosh, M. (eds.): Identity Metasystem Interoperability Version 1.0 (IMI 1.0). OASIS Standard (2009), http://docs.oasis-open.org/imi/identity/v1.0/identity.html
10. Powell, T.A., Schneider, F.: Javascript: The Complete Reference, 2nd edn. McGraw-Hill Osborne Media, Berkeley (2004)
11. Hors, A.L., Hégaret, P.L., Wood, L., Nicol, G., Robie, J., Champion, M., Byrne, S. (eds.): Document Object Model (DOM) Level 2 Core Specification. W3C Recommendation (2000), http://www.w3.org/TR/DOM-Level-2-Core/

Foreign Identities in the Austrian E-Government
An Interoperable eID Solution

Mario Ivkovic and Klaus Stranacher

E-Government Innovation Center (EGIZ), Austria
mario.ivkovic@egiz.gv.at, klaus.stranacher@egiz.gv.at
http://www.egiz.gv.at

Abstract. With the revision of the Austrian E-Government Act [8] in the year 2008, the legal basis for a full integration of foreign persons in the Austrian e-government, has been created. Additionally, the E-Government Equivalence Decree [1] has been published in June 2010. This decree clarifies which foreign electronic identities are considered to be equivalent to Austrian identities and can be electronically registered within the Austrian identity register. Based on this legal framework a concept has been developed which allows non-Austrian citizens to log in to Austrian online administrative procedures using their foreign identity. A solution resting upon this concept has been developed and successfully tested. This solution has become operative in July 2010.

Keywords: E-Government, Interoperability, Electronic Identities.

1 Introduction

Electronic identities (eID) are gaining more and more importance and are a fundamental component of many e-government applications. Due to the mobility of citizens, cross-border interoperability in the European eID landscape has become a key topic. Based on the Directive 1999/93/EC of the European Parliament for digital signatures [7], Member States have developed individual and partly diverging e-government strategies and solutions. Thus, cross-border interoperability turned out to be a challenging issue.

A project dealing with this challenge is STORK (Secure idenTity acrOss boRders linKed), an ICT Policy Support and Competitiveness and Innovation Program (CIP) of the EU with the aim "to establish a European eID Interoperability Platform that will allow citizens to establish new e-relations across borders, just by presenting their national eID"[1]. The results of the work described in this paper, are presently being integrated into the Austrian STORK implementation.

The rest of this paper is structured as follows. The next sub section outlines the Austrian eID concept. The second section gives an overview about the legal basis for foreign identities in Austria. The next section presents an approach for the integration of foreign eIDs into the Austrian e-government. This includes

---

[1] https://www.eid-stork.eu/

E. de Leeuw, S. Fischer-Hübner, L. Fritsch (Eds.): IDMAN 2010, IFIP AICT 343, pp. 31–40, 2010.

the login to Austrian online administrative procedures as well as the electronic registration in the Austrian identity register. Based on this approach existing components have been extended and new components developed. Therefore the fourth section comprises the implementation. In the last section, we finalize the paper with some conclusions.

1.1   Identification in the Austrian E-Government

In the following sections we give an overview about identification and authentication in the Austrian e-government. Legal basis for identification in Austria is the Austrian E-Government Act[8].

SourcePIN. All persons that are registered in Austria (having a permanent or a non-permanent residence in Austria) are listed in the Central Register of Residence (CRR). To each person in this register a unique number, the CRR number[2], is assigned. Due to data protection laws it is not allowed to use this CRR number for e-government applications. Therefore, the so-called *SourcePIN*, which is derived from the citizen's CRR number by using strong cryptographic means (Triple-DES encryption), has been introduced. The SourcePIN may only be stored on a Citizen Card and is thus under the sole control of the citizen. However, even the SourcePIN may never directly be used as identifier in e-government services. Instead, a sector-specific personal identifier has to be derived from the SourcePIN.

For people who want to use Austrian e-government applications but do not have a residence in Austria, the Supplementary Register for natural persons has been established. Similar to the CRR number, all persons in the supplementary register have a unique number. This number is then used to derive a SourcePIN for natural persons without a residence in Austria.

Sector specific PIN. From the very beginning data protection was an integral component of the Austrian e-government strategy. Therefore, the use of cross-departmental identifiers has been avoided. Rather than using the SourcePIN directly, sector specific PINs that are derived from the SourcePIN (applying cryptographic hash functions), must be used. A sector specific PIN (ssPIN) in contrast to a SourcePIN may be stored for further processing. With ssPINs it should be prevented to link a person across different administrative procedures from different departments.

Citizen Card. The Citizen Card is an essential part of the Austrian e-government strategy. A Citizen Card is used for unique identification and authentication of citizens in online procedures of the public administration.

In the Austrian E-Government Act[8] a Citizen Card is defined as a logical unit independent of its technical implementation, which combines a qualified

---

[2] http://www.epractice.eu/en/cases/crraustria

electronic signature with an *Identity Link*. The Identity Link provides a means for identification by linking a qualified certificate with the citizen's SourcePIN.

A Citizen Card can be e.g. a smart card, a mobile phone, or any other device fulfilling the following requirements:

Electronic Signature: A Citizen Card must support qualified electronic signatures as defined in the Austrian Signature Act [2]. Therefore, at least one certificate, which is used for the creation of a qualified electronic signature, is stored on a Citizen Card. Additionally, a further certificate that can be used for signature creation or data encryption may be stored on a Citizen Card.

Identification: With the Identity Link, an XML structure containing the SourcePIN, it is possible to uniquely identify a citizen in an e-government procedure.

Data Storage: A Citizen Card must provide data storage divided into so-called *Info Boxes*. In one of the Info Boxes, the above mentioned Identity Link is stored.

The Identity Link uniquely assigns a Citizen Card to a citizen. This is done by signing an XML structure that contains the citizen's public key(s) and the SourcePIN. The signature is created by the SourcePIN Register Authority[3]. By doing this, the public keys are unambiguously linked to a particular person.

Citizen Card Environment. The Austrian e-government strategy introduced the concept of a Citizen Card Environment (CCE) in order to ease the access to a Citizen Card. The CCE, also referred to as Citizen Card Software (CCS), is thus the middleware between e-government applications and Citizen Cards. A CCE offers functionalities for electronic signature creation and verification, data encryption and decryption, and provides access to the Info Boxes. Currently several different forms of CCEs are available, ranging from software applications running on a client computer to Java-Applets embedded in an e-government web site[4].

Basic Services. In order to kick-start e-government in Austria, the Austrian Federal Chancellery has developed some software components, called Modules for Online Applications (MOA-Modules), which offer useful basic functionalities for e-government application operators. The MOA-Modules are open source and can be used free of charge. At the present time the following modules are available:

MOA-SS: This module provides functionalities for the creation of electronic signatures. Supported are XML signatures according to XMLDSIG [4].

---

[3] The SourcePIN Register Authority is an authority conducted by the Austrian Data Protection Commission, http://www.stammzahlenregister.gv.at/

[4] http://www.buergerkarte.at/en/index.html

MOA-SP: This module offers functionalities for the validation of electronic
signatures. Supported is the validation of XMLDSIG signatures as well as
CMS signatures [5].

MOA-ID: This module provides means for secure identification and authentication of citizens within e-government applications. The unique identification is achieved by reading the Identity Link and the creation of a qualified
signature.

2   Foreign Identities

In the year 2008 the Austrian E-Government Act [8] has been amended. With
this revision the acceptance of foreign identities has been enabled. §6(5) states:

> Data subjects who are not registered in the Central Register of Residents
> nor in the Supplementary Register may be entered in the Supplementary
> Register in the course of an application for the issue of a Citizen Card
> without proof of the data in accordance with paragraph 4 if the appli-
> cation is provided with a qualified electronic signature which is linked
> to an equivalent electronic verification of that person's unique identity
> in his or her country of origin. The Federal Chancellor shall lay down
> by Order further conditions for equivalence. The SourcePIN Authority
> shall, upon application of the data subject, provide the SourcePIN of
> the data subject directly to the Citizen Card enabled application where
> the official procedure is carried out. The SourcePIN may be used by the
> SourcePIN Register Authority only to calculate ssPINs."

As a result foreign electronic identities are fully integrated in the Austrian
e-government in case they are associated with qualified electronic signatures. As
a requirement, if the citizen is not already registered in the Central Register of
Residents (person has a registered residence in Austria), the foreign citizen must
be registered in the Supplementary Register. The SourcePIN Authority is then
able to derive a SourcePIN. So a temporary Identity Link, temporary because this
Identity Link is repeatedly generated and not permanently stored on an eID card,
can be forwarded to an e-government application. The e-government application
uses the Identity Link only for the computation of the sector specific PIN.

With §6(5) of the Austrian E-Government Act the possibility to register a
person electronically has been given. For the concrete usage it must be determined which electronic identity is considered to be equivalent. This is done by
the so called E-Government Equivalence Decree [1]. The decree has been published in June 2010. Thereby it is determined which identification attributes
from a foreign identity must be used. Table 1 gives an overview about the electronic identities which are considered to be equivalent. All this countries have
in common that they have a unique identifier which can be used for identifying
persons. Depending on the country this number is e.g. the tax number, social
insurance number, health care user number or the personal identification number. Usually this identifier is stored in the certificate (as serial number), except

Table 1. Equivalent foreign electronic identities [1]

Country	Unique identifier in the country of origin	Name of the eID card
Belgium	RRN number (Rijksregister-Registre National)	Belgian Personal Identity Card (Elektronische identiteitskaart BELPIC)
Estonia	PIC number (Personal Identification Code)	Estonian ID Card (Isikutunnistus ID-kaart ESTEID)
Finland	FINUID number (Finnish Unique Identifier)	Finnish Electronic Identity Card (FINEID)
Iceland	SSN number (Social Security Number)	Icelandic bank card
Italy	Tax identification number	Electronic Identity Card (Carta d'identità elettronica)
		National Service Card (Carta nazionale dei servizi)
Liechtenstein	Serial number of the certificate in conjunction with PEID number (Personal Identification Number)	lisign
Lithuania	Personal ID code	Lithuanian Personal Identity Card (Asmens Tapatybės Kortelė)
Portugal	Personal identification number	Personal Identity Card (Cartão do Cidadão)
	Social insurance number	
	Tax number	
	Healthcare user number	
Sweden	Personal ID number	Nationellt id-kort
Slovenia	Serial number of the certificate in conjunction with PRN number (Personal Registration Number) or tax identification number	SIGOV Card
	Tax identification number	Halcom ONE FOR ALL!
	Tax identification number	Postarca smart card
Spain	Personal ID number	DNI electronic (DNI electrónico)

Liechtenstein. In this case a national register query must be performed to get the national identifier (see section 4.2 for details).

For the login to an Austrian online application the foreign person must be identified via the Central Register of Residents or the Supplementary Register. For this purpose the available identification attributes are read from the eID card. Based on these attributes, persons can be search in the registers. Additionally, to get registered in the Supplementary Register it is currently needed to go to the local department.

In this paper we will show the concept and implementation of identifying foreign persons in the Austrian e-government. The focus is on the electronic registration in the Supplementary Register according to §6(5) of the Austrian E-Government and the E-Government Equivalence Decree.

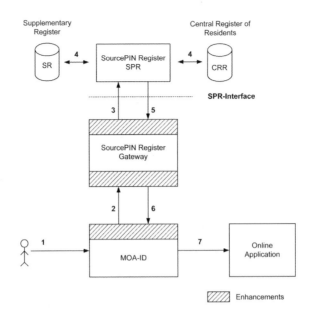

Fig. 1. Foreign Identities in the Austrian E-Government

3 Concept

This section describes the realized concept that enables the login to an Austrian e-government application using a foreign eID card. The following functional description covers the login to a foreign person in case he or she is already registered in the Supplementary Register as well as the person must be registered in the Supplementary Register previously.

Figure 1 shows the process consisting of following steps:

1. A foreign citizen wants to log in to an Austrian e-government application using an eID card. For accessing the application the citizen must be identified and authenticated via the basic service MOA-ID.

   If the citizen wants to login, MOA-ID tries to read the Identity Link from the eID card (via the Citizen Card Environment). This attempt fails, because only Austrian eID cards hold an Identity Link. So MOA-ID detects that the inserted eID card is a foreign one, a non activated Austrian Citizen Card or an unknown signature card. For the following it is assumed that the inserted eID card is a foreign card. This is checked by MOA-ID anyway.

   To get the identification data from the foreign person (e.g. first name, family name and national eID number) the card holder is requested to create a signature. Therefore, a request is sent to the CCE which creates the qualified signature using the actual eID card. This signature is sent back to MOA-ID. Next MOA-ID sends this signature to the SourcePIN Register Gateway (SPR Gateway). This gateway provides a simple access to the SourcePIN Register.

2. The SPR Gateway gets the foreign signature from MOA-ID and verifies it. Thereby also the signatory certificate is checked if it is qualified. In case the certificate is qualified the necessary identification data is extracted. This data are first name, family name, national eID number and information about the certificate (validity, issuer, public key, etc.). For Liechtenstein an additional register query must be performed to get the current national identifier. After collecting all required data a request to the SourcePIN Register is sent.

3. The gateway forwards the request (containing the person data) to the SPR to get the Identity Link of the foreign person.

4. The SPR searches the Central Register of Residents (CRR) and the Supplementary Register (SR). Now the following two cases are distinguished:
   (a) If the foreign person is already registered in one of the two registers an Identity Link can be generated for this person on the fly.
   (b) The foreign person is neither registered in the CRR nor in the SR. In this case the person is electronically registered in the SR based on §6(5) of the E-Government Act. If the registration was successful (the person is now registered in the SR), an Identity Link can be generated. In case the registration failed an appropriate error message is produced.

5. Depending on the prior steps the generated Identity Link or the error message is sent back to the SPR Gateway.

6. Based on the received Identity Link, MOA-ID creates a security token (SAML artifact). Alternatively, if an error message has been received, the message is shown to the person.

7. The person is granted access to the e-government application.

4   Implementation

The concept described has been realized in the course of a project. Therefore existing services (MOA-ID and SPR Gateway) have been extended. In the following sections these enhancements are described. Furthermore, the realization of the register query for Liechtenstein is depicted.

4.1   MOA-ID Enhancements

For the MOA-ID enhancements the current release has been adapted. These adaptions contain following enhancements regarding the integration of foreign eID cards:

– *Foreign eID card*: MOA-ID has been adapted to support foreign eID cards. MOA-ID is now able to detect and support foreign eID cards. This is done via sending a request to the Citizen Card Environment to read the Identity Link from the card. In case of an activated Austrian Citizen Card the Identity Link is returned and the login process proceeds as usual. If a foreign card is in the card reader, an Identity Link could not be found and so an appropriate error message is sent back to MOA-ID. Based on this error message MOA-ID detects, that the inserted card is a foreign one.

– *Signature creation*: To get the signature certificate from the foreign citizen, MOA-ID has been amended to send a request to the Citizen Card Environment. Via this request the citizen is asked to create a signature using his or her qualified certificate. After creation of the signature the Citizen Card Environment sends the signature back to MOA-ID. Finally MOA-ID sends the signature to the SPR Gateway to get the temporary Identity Link of the foreign citizen.
– *Configuration*: The last enhancement concerns the configuration of MOA-ID. In the context of the enhancement new configuration parameters must be defined to enable the access to the SourcePIN Register Gateway.

4.2   SourcePIN Register Gateway

The main purpose of the SourcePIN Register Gateway is to enable a simple and secure access to the SourcePIN Register. Following enhancements have been made: The gateway has been extended by an additional request that can be sent to the SourcePIN Register. This request contains the foreign signature. This signature is then used to get the signatory certificate and so to get the identification data of the foreign citizen. The response of the SPR Gateway contains the generated Identity as result.

In the following the process from receiving the request from MOA-ID till sending back the Identity Link is described in more detail:

1. MOA-ID sends the request to get the Identity Link to the gateway. This request contains the signature of the foreign person.
2. After receiving the signature the SPR Gateway verifies the signature. Additionally a certificate check is executed to check if the certificate is qualified.
3. In case the certificate is qualified the gateway extracts following person data from the certificate:
   (a) First name
   (b) Family name
   (c) Date of birth (optional): Only if available from certificate
   (d) Sex (optional): Only if available from certificate
   (e) Public key
   (f) Travel document:
       i. Document number: This number corresponds to the unique identifier of the country. Usually this identifier is encoded in the certificate, except Liechtenstein (see following sub section for details).
       ii. Document type: Hard coded string *ELEKTR_DOKUMENT* (which means *electronic document*)
       iii. Issue date
       iv. Issuing authority
       v. Issuing country
4. Using the extracted person data a SOAP request (according to the SPR interface specification [3]) is created and sent to the SourcePIN Register. The register evaluates the request and querires the Central Register of Residents

and the Supplementary Register. As search criteria only first name, family name, unique identifier and - if available - the date of birth are used. If the person can be found in one of these registers a temporary Identity Link is created and sent back to MOA-ID. In case the person could not be found, the SourcePIN register adds the person to the Supplementary Register according to §6(5) of the E-Government Act. Thereby, all available person data are stored in the Supplementary Register. After a successful registration an Identity Link can be produced and sent back to the gateway.

5. The gateway forwards the Identity Link, or the error message if an error occurred during the registration process, to MOA-ID.

Liechtenstein. The certificate of Liechtenstein does not contain a unique identifier. Instead the identifier is stored in a central identity register. Together with the federal administration of Liechtenstein we developed a SOAP interface to this register (see also Figure 2). Using this interface the SPR Gateway is able to request for the unique identifier. Thereby the request is an *AttributeQuery* according to the SAML specification [6]. This request contains the qualified certificate of the citizen and is sent to the identity register of Liechtenstein. Based on this certificate the identity register is able to find the person. Then the identity register creates a response containing the unique identifier and additionally the first name, family name and date of birth. This response is sent back to the Austrian SPR Gateway. After receiving the response, the SPR Gateway extracts the person data. Using this data the person can be searched for within the Austrian registers or can be added to the Austrian Supplementary Register.

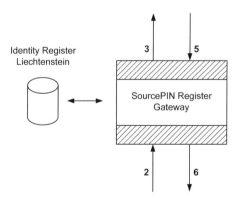

Fig. 2. Register query for Liechtenstein

5   Conclusions

This paper describes how foreign identities are handled within the Austrian e-government. Based on an updated legal framework a solution has been developed which allows non-Austrian citizens to log in to an Austrian online service using their foreign eID. The implementation has been successfully tested and was launched in July 2010.

The presented concept fits very well to the pan-European approach of interoperable electronic identities. Foreign citizen can directly use Austrian e-government services without the need of a prior on-site registration.

However, although the Equivalence Decree currently lists 14 eID cards which are considered to be equivalent, not all off them can be actually used at the present time. This is because not all of these eID card are already implemented in the available Citizen Card Environments. The CCE that mostly supporting foreign eID cards is MOCCA[5]. MOCCA supports the Belgian BELPIC, the Estonian ESTID, the eID card from Liechtenstein and two different eID cards from Italy. The MOCCA team will integrate further eID cards in the near future. Nevertheless, the developed system has already been started.

Future work touches the SIGOV cards of Slovenia. As with the certificate of Liechtenstein, the Slovenian SIGOV card does not contain the national identifier (tax or PRN number). Additionally, in this case no national register can be queried for the identifier. However, the Slovenian government conducts a Web service[6] which is able to verify a given tax or PRN number. Based on this Web service a concept for identifying persons is currently under development.

References

1. Austrian Federal Law Gazette (BGBl) Nr. 170/2010. E-Government Equivalence Decree, Decree of the Federal Chancellor laying down conditions for equivalence under Section 6(5) of the E-Government Act (2010)
2. Bundesgesetzblatt (BGBl) Teil I Nr. 190/1999. Bundesgesetz über elektronische Signaturen (Signaturgesetz – SigG) (1999), available in German only, http://www.ris.bka.gv.at
3. Bundesministerium fuer Inneres, Sektion IV - Support Unit ZMR. SZR 2.0 Anwendungsdokumentation, Version 1.0 (November 2009)
4. Eastlake 3rd, D., Reagle, J., Solo, D.: (Extensible Markup Language) XML-Signature Syntax and Processing (March 2002), http://www.ietf.org/rfc/rfc3275.txt
5. Housley, R.: Cryptographic Message Syntax (CMS) (July 2004), http://www.ietf.org/rfc/rfc3852.txt
6. OASIS. Assertions and Protocols for the OASIS Security Assertion Markup Language (SAML) V2.0 (March 2005)
7. European Parliament and Council. Directive 1999/93/EC of the European Parliament and of the Council of 13 December 1999 on a Community framework for electronic signatures (December 1999), http://eur-lex.europa.eu/LexUriServ/ LexUriServ.do?uri=CELEX:31999L0093:EN:HTML
8. Austrian Federal Law Gazette (BGBl) part I Nr. 10/2004. The Austrian E-Government Act, Federal Act on Provisions Facilitating Electronic Communications with Public Bodies, entered into force on 1 March 2004; amended by BGBl I Nr. 7/2008 (amendments entered into force on 1 January 2008) including the Corrigendum in BGBl I Nr. 59/2008 (2008)

---

[5] http://mocca.egovlabs.gv.at/

[6] Slovenian Web service for verifying a tax or PRN number, https://storitve-ca.gov.si/avtentikacija.htm

Understanding the Economics of Electronic Identity: Theoretical Approaches and Case Studies

Anssi Hoikkanen, Margherita Bacigalupo, Wainer Lusoli,
Ioannis Maghiros, and Stavri Nikolov

European Commission's Joint Research Centre – Institute for Prospective
Technological Studies (JRC-IPTS)
Anssi.HOIKKANEN@ec.europa.eu

Abstract. This paper discusses the economics of electronic identity (eIdentity) from both theoretical and practical perspectives. Personal identity data are becoming increasingly important in online transactions, and they have never been monetised to the extent they are today. Consequently, there is a need for an improved understanding of the economic externalities resulting from the electronic use of identities in transactions. In this context, we distinguish four main theoretical approaches for understanding economics of identity: identity as a consumption good, identity as a capital asset, identity as a social good, and identity as a cost. We analyse each of these approaches in terms of their benefits to understanding economics of identity, their drawbacks, and the bearer of the cost of identity provision. After the theoretical part, we go on to discuss three case studies, BBS, eBay and IdenTrust, and apply an appropriate concept of economics of identity to analyse each business case. Finally, we conclude the paper by discussing the implications that each of the different concepts of economics of identity has for policymakers.

1 Introduction

1.1 Background

Identity as a concept has been known for centuries. In the past identity has often been treated as a social good with some externalities or simply as a cost, but its full economic significance is becoming increasingly apparent. Today, personal identity data are vital to the way Internet services are provided, and to citizens' everyday life. Especially in online transactions, personal identity data are becoming an important enabler of the digital economy. They have a crucial role to play in setting the framework conditions so as to sustain this shift while maximising the benefits for economy and society.

The economic importance of electronic identities is increasing for several reasons. Firstly, electronic identification is today indispensable to ensure access to public and private services – including health, education and security. More and more of the personal sphere is recorded, stored and analysed (for example, in the case of nominal e-ticketing, in which identity tags are attached to transactions that were previously anonymous). Identity transactions are based on an increasing number and variety of identity systems. In the Internet, a heterogeneous system of identity assurance has emerged over time, through a mix of open standardisation, engineering ingenuity and

E. de Leeuw, S. Fischer-Hübner, L. Fritsch (Eds.): IDMAN 2010, IFIP AICT 343, pp. 41–58, 2010.

sheer monopolistic inertia. There is today a plethora of sector specific solutions (based on e.g. SSL encryption, PIN, tokens) and e-services (e.g. based on a PKI infrastructure with either strong or weak authentication).

Secondly, the personal identity data of citizens are being used today in two different ways. The first one is to provide access to information and services; this is the 'authentication function' of identity. In addition, however, the personal identifiers used for authentication leave digital traces that may also be used for other, unintended purposes. Profiling – the attribution of identity based on data mining criteria – both for profit (mainly businesses) and security (mainly governments), is on the rise. Other non-personal identifiers may be linked to personal data (as in the case of IP addresses and object tags), and there may be increasing linking of EU citizens' identity to their online and offline activities.

Thirdly, the number of transactions carried out with personal identity data has grown significantly in the past few years, and will most likely continue to do so. Consequently, businesses are increasingly trying to profit from the use of personal identity data for their own gain. There is a tension between the collection of personal data in business-to-consumer transactions and the respect for consumers' privacy preferences. This presents new challenges for policymakers: how to ensure that business abide by current regulations, addressing the challenges to privacy and data protection, while at the same time supporting the economic development of electronic identities and services based on them. Overall, the purposes for which identity data are used today cover a significantly larger spectrum than just authentication. Most significantly, activities such as targeted advertising, based on collected identity data, are becoming more and more common, and in this context there has been an emergence of numerous profiling models (advertising, crime detection, compliance with rules, health monitoring). The economic attractiveness of such activities is clear; indeed, personal identity data have never been monetised to the extent occurring today. While the economic significance of such activities is largely invisible at the moment, emerging mobile, sensor and social networking technologies facilitate the creation of novel services that, in addition to their other functions, enable users to perceive the economic importance of their electronic identities. Furthermore, as distributed systems are assembled from components that have been created for different purposes, economic incentives are becoming as important as technical design in achieving system dependability; without economic incentives there may not be sufficient motivation for different companies to ensure the compatibility of their applications with large-scale systems.

Due to the economic importance of electronic identity, the economics of identity need to be understood in a much more systematic and formalised way than has traditionally been the case. Relatively little is known about how identities are used in economic transactions (either as an enabler or as part of the transaction), what is the economic value of the identity data, how it could be measured, and what business models support the use of electronic identity. This analysis is necessary to quantify the economic significance of the identity market, and to understand how the dynamics of the identity markets function. It is only through this understanding that policymakers are able to effectively regulate the identity space. The drawback of analysing economics of identity in this sense is that to date, there is no clearly defined framework for this analysis; therefore it would take policymakers a significant amount of additional effort to carry out this task reliably and in appropriate detail.

In this paper, the term eIdentity is used to indicate a set of personal information and data relevant to a human's identity (personal and/or collective identity data) when stored and transmitted via electronic systems, including but not limited to computer networks. The terms electronic identity, digital identity and eID are also used to the same purpose in the literature.

1.2 Research Questions

Evidently, there is a clear need for improved understanding of the economic externalities of electronic identification. A much more detailed analysis is needed of how exactly identity functions as an economic object, what kind of consequences this has both from a theoretical perspective and for policymakers, and how these consequences can be efficiently managed and regulated. To gain a fuller understanding of these issues, we need a framework that looks into the economics from various angles, distinguishes between different ways of understanding them, and looks at how they can be applied in different business contexts.

We foresee that different concepts of economics of identity can be classified into distinct approaches, or schools of thought. Each of them will have different consequences in terms of how identity is defined as an economic object, and how the associated economic externalities can be analysed. Further, each approach has its own set of benefits and drawbacks, with regard to what kind of analysis it allows; researching these benefits and limitations provides an overview of the different issues and considerations that must be taken into account. In order to arrive at a fuller understanding of the economics of identity, it is necessary to map out the various economically relevant aspects of eIdentity.

We therefore propose the following research questions that this paper seeks to answer: 1) What approaches to economics of identity can be identified? 2) How does each of them contribute to our understanding of the economics of eIdentity? 3) How can these approaches be applied to existing companies in the marketplace? 4) In light of all this, what kind of policy implications does this raise for policymakers?

2 Ways of Understanding Economics of Identity

In this chapter, we discuss four possible approaches to understand economics of identity by defining each, describing the challenges each one solves, discussing their limitations, providing an example of how each approach can be applied, and finally by concluding how this approach helps us understand economics of identity.

2.1 Identity as a Consumption Good

One way to grasp the economics of identity is to analyse **identity as a consumption good**, in which case users choose their identity according to how and where they want to use it [1]. In this case, identity results from *explicit* choices by the individual. This implies that personal identity data are transactable and can be sold, either temporarily or permanently. In turn, this understanding of identity raises questions of what purposes identity can be used for, how long it remains valid for, and what contractual regimes would be applicable. Identity could also be stolen; this raises issues concerning trust in the transaction environment, accountability, individual responsibility, and appropriate adoption of identity. The classic economic approach to analyse identity as a consumption good is economics of choice. Identity can then be analysed by introducing it as a factor in the utility function as in general economics [2].

'Identity as a consumption good' provides several insights into how these economics function. First, it describes in detail how identities can be used in economic transactions and the possible value of identity in such transactions. Second, the approach allows taking into consideration the fact that people have different identities in different situations and use cases, and that personal identity data can be used in varying ways according to the context. Thus this approach goes a long way towards explaining why the value of the person's identity or personal identity data can differ significantly in varying circumstances. Third, it also brings to the fore the *active role* that the user may have in managing her personal data: as the user chooses which data are the most relevant to the context. The economic consequences that result from this choice of personal data, and the level of personal responsibility required from the user, vary according to the type of data.

Despite the above described assets, this approach has some clear limitations. The approach is quite complex and to accurately determine the value of identity in a particular case would be very difficult. It would be necessary to have a detailed understanding of the case in question and would mean that a lot of data is at the disposal of the stakeholder assessing the value of the identity. The approach also places a heavy burden on the user: the user may have to not only collect and manage, but to process large amounts of information to make informed decisions.

As a consequence of these limitations, the resultant identity markets would likely be very complex, as the circumstances in which identities are used can vary immensely. This would probably lead to inequity between stakeholders and inefficiency in the market. The problem could also be exacerbated by the technical constraints of the transaction environment. Secondly, this approach may require too much effort or access to information on the part of the users: not everyone will be active enough, or well-informed enough, to adequately manage her personal identity data in all circumstances. The most ICT-savvy users would possibly be ready and willing to manage this information, but this would not be the case for all users. Thirdly, there is a significant contrast between user-stated privacy attitudes and their actual privacy-related behaviour. In general, it may be unreasonable to expect complete individual rationality in the context of online transactions. Models of self-control problems and immediate gratification studied by some scholars may offer more realistic descriptions of users' decision-making processes, and explain why even individuals who genuinely want to protect their privacy might not do so. These risks become even higher when the individuals concerned do not perceive the risks resulting from not protecting their privacy as significant [3].

As an example of the contrast between user attitudes and user behaviour, Acquisti et al. have conducted an experiment for two scenarios: willingness to pay for protecting personal information, and willingness to accept a proposal to sell information. Their results show a clear preference for money over data across the vast majority of participants in both information protection and information release scenarios, even when the monetary advantage is low. In addition, the average willingness to accept (the second case) is dramatically higher than the average willingness to protect [4].

Acquisti et al. have also studied why consumers do not always act as rational agents. Their research confirms that consumers often lack enough information to make privacy-sensitive decisions and, even with sufficient information, are likely to trade off long-term privacy for short-term gains. The three most important reasons for consumers not to act rationally are incomplete information, bounded rationality (inability to process and act on vast amounts of data), and systematic psychological deviations from rationality. The latter includes the tendency to favour immediate gratification to future benefit, the possibility to avoid loss being more important than the possibility to win a profit (of the same magnitude), notions of altruism, and fairness instead of private gain [5].

Spiekermann et al. conducted an experiment in which they compared the self-reported privacy preferences of 171 participants with their actual behaviour during an online shopping episode. Their findings suggest that current approaches such as legislation to protect user privacy may not do so effectively, since they assume that consumers are privacy conscious and act accordingly. In the study it was found that most people did not live up to their self-reported preferences, and in fact tended to respond to the majority of questions asked from them during an online shopping session, even if they were highly personal. The varying privacy statements on different websites had no impact on the type of information disclosed. This suggests that people are prone to disregard privacy concerns once engaged in a transaction [6].

To conclude, to deal with identity as a consumption good contributes to our understanding of economics of identity according to classical and behavioural economics. It is market-centric: the cost of identity provision can be understood to be borne by the market, i.e. the highest bidder will manage "my" identity. A significant drawback of this approach is that it requires some idealised assumptions about user behaviour, and how users behave in real life may not conform with theory.

2.2 Identity as a Capital Asset

We can also discuss **identity as a capital asset**. In this case, identity is regarded a property that can be publicly traded. Identity will have a changing value over time and space, because people's valuation of their identity changes with time and social context. When identity is understood as property, the value of pieces (i.e. value of identity in different contexts) does not equal the value of the ensemble. Therefore, the changing value of identity is considered both over time (time inconsistency in value of identity, deferred rewards) and over space (people value their identity differently in different social spaces, use of identity changes the value of identity).

In common with the understanding of identity as a consumption good, 'identity as a capital asset' recognises the changing value of identity data in different use contexts. It also allows for the time value of identity, recognizing the fact that the same person may place a drastically different value on his personal identity data purely because time has passed and this information has a different value in the new situation. This approach also recognises the fact that the value of identity can change when it is used, and may increase or decrease in value depending on the changes caused by the use.

Understanding identity as a capital asset carries with it a number of challenges. Firstly, there are obvious difficulties in measuring the value. There is also the risk of misrepresentation. This may occur through an erroneous combination of parts of the whole by not recognizing all value-generating aspects of identity, or by considering only the most recent information and ignoring what was done a long time ago. We must also take into account the difficulties in predicting future behaviour, which mean that to estimate the value of identity in future carries with it a large inherent risk. All these challenges mean that to analyse identity as a capital asset, though in theory feasible, can in practice result in unreliable estimates of its value.

However, the *dynamics* of identity as a capital asset can be studied through behavioural economics and game theory. In his paper, Cave (2004) discusses the economics of trust according to some simple game theoretic models of specific aspects of trust, in order to analyse how balanced and efficient they are. He discusses the potential tension between efficiency and equilibrium, both in terms of the prevalence of trust behaviour and the network of relationships to which the need to trust others gives rise. In addition, he seeks to identify conditions under which different levels of trust may be widespread and conditions under which a diversity of behaviour is likely. One unexpected consequence of the latter conditions is the existence of 'catastrophes' – discontinuous jumps in the level of trust in response to small changes in underlying conditions [7]. Acquisti et al. have also carried out trust modelling for online transactions. The increasing amount of spam, phishing and other attacks increase users' uncertainty over the consequences of their actions and their distrust towards other online parties. From this starting point, they have developed a theoretical model to represent and compare the online trust decision processes of users, though they do not give any direct results of user behaviour [8]. Furthermore, Ba et al. have discussed the problem of uncertain quality in electronic commerce transactions. They investigate how the trust necessary for online exchange of products and services can be promoted when individuals have short-term temptations to cheat. As a solution, they propose a design of an economic incentive mechanism that serves to encourage consumer confidence in conducting online business transactions [9].

On the whole, understanding identity as a capital asset is a valuable addition to theory, especially with regard to changes in the value of identity according to its use and the passing of time. It also helps us understand the dynamics of economics of identity in different use contexts. A significant limitation is that it requires a very high amount of data to yield accurate results about the economic value of identity. It is worth noting that when we deal with identity as a capital asset, the cost of identity provision rests primarily with the individual. In this respect, this approach clearly differs from understanding identity as a consumption good.

2.3 Identity as a Social Good

The third way to analyse economics of **identity** is **as a social good** (where the esteem and reputation of a person have economic externalities). In this case, identity (or to be more precise, aspects of the personal identity data of individuals) is understood to have network effects, meaning that identity increases in economic value by its increased use (by companies, by people). If identity is understood as a social good, one question to ask if identity is to be publicly provided, and as such cannot be used in transactions. In this case, it would mean that identity is permanent: one (nationally provided) identity would stay with the citizen for the duration of his life. Another possibility for the provision of identity is that it be provided by a collective of persons or organisations. This would mean expanding the concept of identity to groups, i.e. not only individuals, but also social networks composed of individuals would have identities of their own. New research activity has emerged around analysing social networks and studying "communities of interest"; this research field has largely been driven forward by sociologists, though there is also relevant work by economists such as Amartya Sen [10]. 'Identity as a social good' can most gainfully be applied to social networking sites (SNSs) such as Facebook and mySpace.

Identity as a social good is a valuable point of view especially because it provides tools to understand the *network effects* of personal identity data. It gives insights into how the value of identity increases as more people use it, and as it becomes more widely diffused. It gives us a means to analyse how SNSs actually function from an economic point of view, by explaining the means through which they provide economic value to their users. The central concept here is that of *reputation*: how other people's perception of what you are like affects their relations with you, and the resulting economic value of these relations.

While this understanding of identity has several advantages, there are also some moot points. First, it leaves unclear the role of the identity provider. As discussed above, if it is provided publicly, identity cannot then be analysed as a transactional good. It would also be unclear whether identity would be a permanent or temporary one; hence, this understanding leaves open questions of the time value of identity. Second, this approach does not address questions of collective identity, or what their dynamics would be like. To understand the collective aspects of identity is essential to any comprehensive analysis of identity, since so many of today's transactions are carried out between groups or organisations, not individuals.

Some research exists on what kind of information citizens wish to share and what they wish to keep to themselves. For example, Varian has argued that consumers will *rationally* want certain kinds of information about themselves to be available to the public, but other types not (e.g. financially sensitive information). Varian says that there are cases where there is a public interest in having some personal information publicly available; making information available about owners of motor vehicles may ensure their safer operation. In these cases, the public does not really care about *your* personal information, but desires access to the information because it is relevant to *their* interests [11].

Overall, analysing identity as a social good brings valuable contributions to our understanding as it introduces network effects and the changing value of identity (according to esteem and reputation) into the discussion. However, by itself this is not sufficient, as the analysis for the most part does not take into account the transactional nature of identity. Further, when we discuss identity as a social good, its value increases with its diffusion in the network, while its cost stays the same; in other words, the more you use your identity data, the more added value you are able to gain from it. This has a tendency to boost the use of the data by citizens, thereby contributing to the growth of the market. However, as the use of identity data increases, so do the associated problems.

2.4 Identity as a Cost

Finally, the conventional way to understand **identity** is purely **as a cost**. This means that the economic value of identity is only recognized as far as it incurs costs for the different stakeholders (governments, companies, consumers). For example, the costs of privacy enhancing technologies have been studied in this context. Another possibility is to look at costs of identity theft: what is the economic loss, both direct and indirect, caused by the theft of people's online identities. Governments, for example, incur huge infrastructure costs to protect their identity management systems from unauthorised access. In this approach to economics of identity, the concept of cost has at least two meanings: the cost of what people have lost, or the cost they have to pay in order to protect their identity.

The key benefit of this approach is that it allows us to distinguish and study the various identity related costs. The main limitation is equally obvious: the identity related benefits are not considered. However, the costs associated with identity are much easier to estimate than the gains, which makes studying them worthwhile, if only to help us understand how much identity related transactions would have to contribute to the economy to offset the related costs. Therefore, the cost of identity provision will most likely be borne by the market, through the benefits brought about by increased security and control.

As an example, some scholars have studied the cost of privacy breaches in terms of their impact on the company's market value. These studies show that there is a negative correlation between data breaches and the company's market value. Although initially significant, the effect decreases and loses statistical significance rather quickly (even within days), suggesting that the public will quite rapidly recover its confidence in the company [12].

Another example of analysing identity as a cost is the economics of malicious software (malware). While its origins clearly lie in criminal behaviour, some scholars have argued that the magnitude and impact of the malware threat have also been influenced by the decisions and behaviour of legitimate market players such as ISPs, software providers, hardware vendors and consumers. Namely, in many cases these stakeholders may not be adequately incentivised to operate in ways that contribute to the highest possible security, and there may even be market-based incentive mechanisms that contribute to misuse of information. For example, it is often very easy for companies to collect information about their customers, their preferences, habitual ways of using the system, and so on; while this information may be appropriately used by, financially beneficial for, the company in question, there is always the possibility of a third party finding out this information and using it for illegal purposes [13].

In this context, Laudon (1997) has studied market mechanisms of pricing information. He posits that the crisis in the privacy of personal information is a result of market failure, not rapid technological development. He believes this to be a market failure, which has occurred as a result of a poor allocation of personal property rights: the collector of the information has too many rights, the individuals concerned too few. While the financial rewards for privacy invasion can be huge for companies, the individuals do not understand how their personal data will be used, the means of individuals for obtaining information about the use of data are limited, and the costs of finding out this information can be very high [14].

Hann et al. (2002) have studied the value of information privacy in the presence of potential benefits from sharing personal information. They found that the potential benefits, both direct monetary rewards and future convenience, significantly affect user preferences in relation to the use of websites with different privacy policies. They also investigated the monetary value of website privacy protection, and estimated that among US subjects in September 2002, the value of protection against errors, improper access, and secondary use of personal information is between $30 and $45 per person annually [15].

Furthermore, Andrew Odlyzko has studied security as a component of a complex economy (not as an isolated good). In his view, it follows that security can never be optimally effective, but instead will always be subject to severe constraints created by other parts of the economy. He further argues that the interactions of human society and human nature suggest that security will continue to be applied as an afterthought, not as a primary design goal of ICT systems. Therefore, it would be most productive to think of security not as a way to provide ironclad protection, but as the equivalent of speed bumps, which decrease the velocity and impact of electronic attacks to a level where other protection mechanisms can operate [16].

On the whole, the definition of identity as a cost does not really deal with identity, but more with privacy and data protection. The positive, i.e. value-generating, effects of identity are not taken into account, which makes this definition somewhat unsatisfactory. However, this approach can be used to highlight the fact that the cost of identity provision could (and probably should) be borne by the associated benefits such as increased security and better control of the use of identities.

2.5 Summary of Different Approaches

In the table below we summarise the benefits and limitations of each approach to economics of identity, with special emphasis on the consequences that each one has for the analysis of economic externalities.

Table 1. Benefits and drawbacks of various approaches to understanding economics of identity

	Consumption good	Capital asset	Social good	Identity as a cost
Benefits for analysis	Identity as a transactional good: different externalities depending on type of transaction

Changing value of identity according to context: identity as a 'market good'

Identity chosen and managed by the user, who gains control and | Identity as a transactional good: economic externalities vary depending on type of transaction and user actions

Changing value of identity according to context: identity traded in the public marketplace

Time value of identity: time factor can be | Economics of esteem and reputation: analyses the economic value of how we (our identities) are appreciated by others

Network effects of identity: explains how increased use and recognition of identity contribute to the economic value | Distinguishes between different identity related costs and explains how each affects the identity's value

Provides estimates of costs for privacy enhancing software, online fraud, identity theft etc. |

Table 1. (*continued*)

	ownership A solid theoretical basis from classical economics	introduced to economic analysis Changing value of identity according to its use; helps understand fluctuations in value of identity Recognises that value of pieces =/ value of all; value can be measured in specific cases without analysing others	of the system Analysis of economics of SNSs; how do such companies generate value?	
Draw-backs	Results in very complex identity markets; hence limited possibilities to understand and regulate the market Requires significant effort from user; what are the user liabilities in case of misuse of identity? Privacy paradox: users are less concerned by their privacy than they claim to be	Difficulties in measurement; possible lack of reliable financial data Difficulties in recognising all value-generating aspects of identity; a lot of groundwork to be done before economic analysis Requires many assumptions about users' future behaviour	Does not clearly define the role of identity provider: it is not clear who controls the identity data and how, and how they will be affected by economic externalities Does not address collective identities	Only analyses the costs, not the value-generating aspects of identity; thus the analysis will only provide "half a picture"
Cost to provide identity	Will be borne by market or company, enabling the use of more advanced e-services	Will be borne by user, who retains control and ownership	Bearer unclear; should decrease the more identity is used	Should be offset by increased security, control, etc.

3   Case Studies

In this chapter, we analyse the activities of three companies as practical examples of how different approaches to economics of identity can be used to understand the identity market. For our analysis, we have chosen BBS, eBay and IdenTrust because they have three clearly different product and service offerings and three distinct ways of operation. BBS is used to illustrate identity as a consumption good, eBay identity as a social good and IdenTrust identity as a cost.

3.1   BBS Global Validation Service [17]

BBS is a Nordic company offering identity solutions to manage risks and provide certification services. Their service offering includes managed public key infrastructure (PKI), managed one-time passwords, validation services, smartcards, and tokens. These services are accepted by several government organisations in addition to the marketplace, which distinguishes them from other similar services. This is a significant development, given that governments in general are very wary of accepting commercial credentials and instead prefer to rely on their own solutions. As the security standards of the commercial products are constantly improving, this lack of acceptance may be more of an issue of suitability of commercial credentials for governmental purposes, rather than concerns about their lack of reliability.

In general terms, international companies need to handle the complexity of verifying different kinds of signatures and to validate certificates from various issuers worldwide. This is the main challenge that BBS seeks to address. They offer validation services that seek to solve the complex problem of offering signature verification and certificate validation as a service for the receiving party. In this way, their customer can obtain a solution designed to manage different signatures and certificates worldwide. Effective use of digital signatures, especially across national frontiers, reduces costs and complexity of using PKI in global e-business. The service also effectively helps to connect different closed eID communities. Ultimately, BBS aims to function as a single, independent trust provider, which offers one set of standards and one software package for processing of signatures and certificates, as well as effective risk management for using PKI in global business transactions.

BBS operates in two distinct segments of the eIdentity market: they offer multi-purpose ID schemes for heterogeneous citizen-merchant markets, and tailored PKI solutions, with more stringent security parameters, whose users are typically enterprise customers with transactions taking place in closed environments [18]. The most important product of BBS is the Identity Management Platform. Developed in 2008, it is used for issuing, managing and using digital certificates online. It can handle different Certificate Authority (CA) platforms and validation technologies, thereby providing BBS with the flexibility to adapt their certification to the specific needs of individual customers and transactions. The BBS Identity Manager is used to provide all their identification services, including enterprise PKI, mobile PKI, EU-qualified and standard certificates. It can also be used to provide one-time passwords and validation of individual transactions. Because of these characteristics, the BBS Identity Management Platform works well as an example of identity as a consumption good. The service incorporates the nature of identity as a transactional good, something that can easily play one role in a certain context and a different one in another. Moreover, these services take into account the changing value of identity depending on the type of transaction, and accordingly there are different types and levels of security for specific transactions as appropriate. In general, BBS services have been developed with a modular design, allowing their customers to choose the most appropriate combination of identification mechanisms.

The activities of BBS in these markets are complemented by their participation in international expert groups such as European Committee for Banking Standards (Mobile Payments Workgroup) and Mobey Forum (Mobile Authentication and Business Ecosystem), and standardisation groups such as European Payment Council (EPC) and European Committee for Banking Standards (ECBS). Their participation in these bodies enables them to offer identity solutions that fit better with specific use cases and transactions, as well as influence the future development of the industry.

When we analyse identity as a consumption good, identity is something chosen and managed by the user. In the BBS case, the customer company gains control and ownership of the certified identity, enabling them to manage the identity according to their particular needs. This also means that the customer company can use several identities and sets of identity data. In this situation, it is obvious that the value of identity depends on the transaction and context it is used in; the identity may even be part of the transaction itself, as befits this school of thought, though this is not explicitly specified by BBS.

Even though the customer company manages its own identity, we must bear in mind that BBS, as the identity provider, has a large role in assisting the customer choose the form of identity to be used. This may in practice lessen the influence that the customer company has over the choice and use of their identity. However, it is always the customer who makes the ultimate decision, with BBS having just an advisory and supportive role. The large role of the provider may also be an advantage: as discussed in this paper, one of the key drawbacks of analysing identity as a consumption good is that it requires significant effort from the user, but in this particular case the effort is mediated by BBS.

The activities of BBS also go some way towards addressing the privacy paradox: although users are generally less conscious of their information security than they claim to be, a company such as BBS helps them see the risks more clearly and manage them appropriately. We might even say that such companies are *needed* because their customers don't understand the risks well enough. Hopefully, this state of affairs will change over time as both personal and business users become more conscious of the benefits and risks associated with online identification; however, at the moment, companies like BBS still have a useful role to play/

In the business model of BBS, the cost of identity provision rests with the customer companies, as they need the electronic identities to provide their financial services. Generally, these companies are able to charge these costs from their own customers in the form of service fees and the like, so ultimately the cost of identity provision rests with the market. In this way, too, the BBS services deal with identity as a consumption good.

3.2   eBay [19]

eBay is a US-based company specialising in online auctions and sale of nearly any type of merchandise. In eBay, each seller has his own profile that is rated by the people who have bought products from this particular seller. The most highly rated sellers acquire the status of "Power Seller", while lowly rated sellers may be excluded from eBay altogether. In this way, eBay closely resembles any social networking site with significant user interaction and rating of individual users by their peers.

The key to operations of eBay is the economics of reputation. It is not possible for the buyer to directly examine the product, and so he must rely on whatever information he can get of the seller when deciding on how to bid. The way a particular seller handles his sales, how reliably he ships the purchases, how promptly he answers requests from information, and so on, all affect his rating in eBay. Therefore the identity of a user has a particular value in eBay; the higher the rating, the higher the value of user identity. This is in line with considering identity as a social good.

Several studies have been made on how to quantify the value of the identity in eBay. Resnick et al. conducted an experiment in which a high-reputation, established eBay dealer sold matched products both under his regular identity and under new seller identities, which were in reality also operated under him. As predicted, the established identity fared better. They found that the difference in buyers' willingness-to-pay was 8.1% of the selling price. They then conducted a second experiment in the same format, but compared sales by relatively new sellers with and without negative feedback. Surprisingly, they found out that one or two negative feedbacks for the new sellers did not affect willingness-to-pay [20]. Melnik et al. have made a similar empirical study of the value of the seller's reputation in eBay. Their conclusion is that the seller's reputation has a positive and statistically significant, but small, impact on the price [21].

The rating structure of eBay generates network effects, which are a cornerstone of understanding identity as a social good. As the ratings of individual sellers change, the ones with higher ratings are likely to attract more business with regard to peers who have the same product. If users buy more from a particular seller because of his high rating and are satisfied, they may then rate the seller highly, boosting his rating yet again. Conversely, low ratings may generate distrust and a tendency to rate a seller lowly even if he does not "really" deserve it, thus creating a polarising effect. People tend not to form their opinions in a vacuum, but instead rely heavily on the opinions and prejudices of other people. These network effects are often magnified online, as people have access to the opinions and experiences of a much higher number of people than would be possible in the physical world. In effect, eBay functions as a trusted third party who "guarantees" the credit ratings of individual sellers. By providing its credit rating information, they give buyers and sellers the confidence to trade with unknown trading partners, improving market liquidity [22].

When analysing identity as a social good, a significant drawback is that it often leaves some important questions unanswered. For instance, it does not address the question of collective identities; in eBay, by analogue, there is no possibility for such an actor as a "collective seller". Similarly, the eBay example can only be used to understand the economic value of identities of individual actors. Also, there may be issues of too strict or too lenient ratings by buyers, meaning that two sellers with similar products cannot be directly compared [23].

In this particular school of thought, the bearer of the cost of identity provision is not specified. However, in the eBay business model the bearer of this cost is very clear, as it rests squarely with the user. This is the case because eBay charges a fee both for placing an item for sale and for each transaction, generating income according to economic value and number of products.

3.3 IdenTrust [24]

IdenTrust is a technology provider whose main product is a PKI-based identification system, used both by governments and private companies, with the finance sector as their main client. They issue credentials and provide a supporting infrastructure including operational, technological and legal services. The IdenTrust credentials are designed to provide three key capabilities: authentication (provision of identity), encryption (safeguarding content, eliminating unauthorised access) and digital signing (user-level signatures of specific transactions).

The IdenTrust credentials are designed to provide three key capabilities: authentication (provision of identity), encryption (safeguarding content, eliminating unauthorised access) and digital signature (user-level signatures of specific transactions). In addition, IdenTrust credentials are designed to comply with relevant anti-money laundering or other anti-abuse regulations (i.e. Sarbanes-Oxley and HIPAA health data regulations).

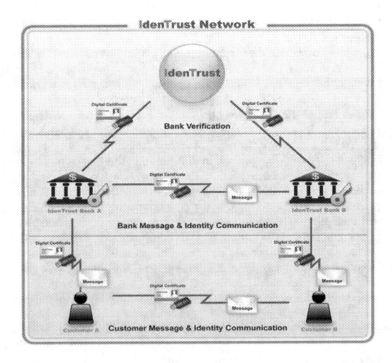

Fig. 1. Functioning of the IdenTrust Trust Network
(source: IdenTrust, ref. #25)

IdenTrust products enable companies make authentication an integral part of their business processes and so to be able to conduct their operations reliably and securely over the Internet beyond fulfilling their legal obligations. IdenTrust products rely on an open standard that can be used by financial institutions to gain interoperability and legal acceptance in 120 countries. The membership of the IdenTrust network is restricted to institutions that agree to abide by the conditions set by IdenTrust, thereby ensuring that the standard is utilised in an appropriate manner. IdenTrust policies govern who receives the identity and how each individual or business is vetted to guarantee they really are who they say they are, along with making certain that the process is done consistently everywhere around the world. IdenTrust identities encrypt and control the process flows, in order to prevent the interception of a transaction, in this way combating phishing and man-in-the-middle attacks.

The Trust Network operates as follows. It first specifies how a digital identity certificate can be issued and how it is validated. The transaction data and signed certificate are exchanged between the stakeholders involved in the transaction. The messages related to the transaction data are exchanged between the customers on either end of the transaction. IdenTrust only validates the identities used by these customers, not the data associated with the transaction. The transaction data itself is never passed to IdenTrust; the only information IdenTrust receives and sends back to the banks is validation of participant identities. All individuals and systems using the network are identified using IdenTrust digital certificates [25].

Overall, IdenTrust supplies the technology and legal mechanisms to let Internet trading partners trust in another's identity. This enables their customer companies to use the Internet to open new markets, reduce transaction costs and create auditable records of their transactions. Hence the costs incurred by identity products are ultimately beneficial or even necessary for such companies, even if they at first look appear as a cost alone [26].

Nevertheless, the primary benefit of analysing the IdenTrust products and services is that it helps us understand in detail the economics of identity as a cost. The IdenTrust products differentiate between costs associated with electronic identification: the PKI technology itself, infrastructure, support services, service setup and management, as well as specific transactions for which credentials are needed. In addition, the IdenTrust products can also be used to provide estimates of the costs more specific identity related issues, such as protection against online fraud, or the setup of an account for a particular purpose. Once the different types of identity related costs are distinguished, they become easier to quantify, though arriving at exact figures remains very challenging.

The obvious drawback of looking at identity just as a cost is that the positive value of the identification services is, quite often, not fully recognised. Instead, it is taken (almost) for granted that companies will need to purchase these services as a regular part of their operations. While this may be true, this lack of recognition of the value-generating aspects of identity could mean that companies such as IdenTrust are unable to fully capitalise on the economic possibilities of electronic identity. Hence, we can say that looking at identity from a pure cost perspective is viable only as a partial approach. It is helpful in assessing the related costs, but to arrive at a fuller understanding of economics of identity, methods and insights from other schools of thought are also needed.

In this approach, the cost of its provision will be paid for by companies purchasing the services from IdenTrust, but will ultimately be charged to their customers. Whether the client companies need an electronic identity of a certain kind and level of security to comply with governmental regulations, to satisfy their customers' expectations, or to be able to run their operations more efficiently and attract more business, the advantages brought about by the services offset the cost of the identification services. Therefore the economic benefits of the eIdentity services are always implicitly recognised.

4   Conclusions for Policymakers

It is evident that the various economic approaches allocate a different, but by itself incomplete, function to identity as an economic object. Consequently, we believe that none of the approaches suffices by itself to analyse economics of identity in a satisfactory way. Instead, this can only be achieved by combining the understandings and methodologies of each one.

Each of the schools of thought has specific consequences for regulators and other policymakers, both on a national and European level. As discussed above, the traditional approach is to treat identity as a cost. This has the advantages of **making policymakers aware of the magnitude of identity-related costs** as well as the fact that there must be significant benefits to render positive the overall economics of deploying identity infrastructures. There is a wide variety of economically significant identity, privacy and data protection issues, recognised by identity management companies such as IdenTrust, and who seek to address these issues through their product portfolios, including the identification and measurement of the various associated costs. By following the activities of such companies and the markets they address, it becomes **easier for policymakers to monitor the various identity related costs in different markets,** and consequently formulate suitable policy actions in each of them.

Understanding identity as a consumption good or as a capital asset both have the advantage of **emphasizing the *transactional* role of identity**. In many transactions, it is not necessary or even appropriate to link a participant to a transaction with a specific living individual. For example, in cash transactions, the buyer only has to be in possession of a sufficient amount of money, not to reveal her identity; while in other cases it may be necessary for either the buyer or the seller to identify herself. In yet other transactions, identities themselves form a part of the transaction. Companies such as BBS function as identity providers for all these different types of transactions, while their customer is the stakeholder that ultimately remains in control of (and responsible for) the actual use of the identities. What this means for policymakers is that they have to be prepared to recognise the various ways in which personal identity data is used in different transactions, and be ready to adopt regulatory measures most suitable to each particular situation.

However, one difficulty with this understanding of economics of identity is that it is not always easy for users to understand how their personal identity data are used. This issue is made more serious by the privacy paradox: the fact that users are in practice not as conscious of privacy implications of transactions as they claim to be.

This is already partly addressed by BBS and other identity providers: these companies offer identity management and support services precisely because their customers need advice on how to manage their identities and identity data more securely and efficiently. However, as valuable as the corrective actions within the marketplace are, these issues also need to be addressed by policymakers. They should **make it as easy as possible for business and citizens to manage their personal information**. This can take place by improving citizen awareness, by providing them accurate and reasonably detailed (but not overly so) information about electronic identities and personal data management, and by making it necessary for companies to clearly disclose their privacy policies and practices.

Analysing identity as a capital asset has the particular advantage of acknowledging the various roles, and hence economic values, that an electronic identity can have depending on the situation. As the value of identity changes according to the extent of its use and the passing of time, so do the ways in which the identity generates value. However, this granularity complicates things for policymakers: it can be difficult just to recognise all the different roles of identity, let alone to reliably measure the monetary value that each one may have. It is therefore **necessary for policymakers to create appropriate tools**, both conventional and novel, **to measure the value of identity in different situations**. This should include the monitoring and quantitative analysis of the activities of the major players in the marketplace, including IdenTrust and BBS. Only this makes it possible to accurately analyse identity as a capital asset.

Finally, when identity is considered as a social good, the main benefit that emerges from this approach is **recognising the economic value of identity in social networks**. By analysing how and why the value of identity increases as more stakeholders become aware and use it in transactions, for example in the business models of eBay and other online retail companies, policymakers become more conscious of the ways in which the identity of one stakeholder can interact with those of others, and how these interactions create value in the whole network. However, for this kind of analysis to be possible, it has to be clearly defined who the provider of identity actually is (e.g. state or private, which private stakeholder), and how the identity can in practice be used in transactions. The eBay business model is again useful for understanding these issues better, because it very clearly demarcates the roles and varying responsibilities of buyers, sellers and the service provider itself.

Reference

1. Akerlof, G.A., Kranton, R.E.: Economics and Identity. Quarterly Journal of Economics 115.3 (2000)
2. Fine, B.: The Economics of Identity and the Identity of Economics? Cambridge Journal of Economics Advance Access (October 26, 2008); Davis, J.B.: Akerlof and Kranton on Identity in Economics: Inverting the Analysis. Cambridge Journal of Economics 31.3 (2007)
3. Acquisti, A.: Privacy in Electronic Commerce and the Economics of Immediate Gratification, H. John Heinz III School of Public Policy and Management, Carnegie Mellon University, vol. 1
4. Acquisti, A., Grossklags, J.: When 25 Cents Is Too Much: An Experiment on Willingness-to-Sell and Willingness-to-Protect Personal Information. In: Workshop on the Economics of Information Security 2007, vol. 1 (2007)

5. Acquisti, A., Grossklags, J.: Privacy and Rationality in Individual Decision-Making. In: Workshop on the Economics of Information Security 2004, vol. 1 (2004)
6. Spiekermann, S., Grossklags, J., Berendt, B.: E-Privacy in 2nd Generation E-Commerce: Privacy Preferences Versus Actual Behavior. In: Electronic Commerce Conference 2001, Tampa, USA, vol. 1 (2001)
7. Cave, J.: The Economics of Trust between Cyber Partners. ForeSight - UK Department for Innovation, Universities and Skills, London (2004); Also Cave, J., Marsden, C.: Quis Custodiet Ipsos Custodes in the Internet: Self-Regulation as a Threat and a Promise. In: 36th Research Conference on Communication, Information and Internet Policy, George Mason University School of Law, Arlington, VA, September 26-28, vol. 1 (2008)
8. Acquisti, A.: Trust Modelling for Online Transactions: A Phishing Scenario. In: Privacy, Security, Trust Conference 2006, vol. 1 (2006)
9. Ba, S., Whinston, A., Zhang, H.: Building Trust in the Electronic Market through an Economic Incentive Mechanism. In: International Conference on Information Systems, vol. 1 (1999)
10. Sen, A.: Identity and Violence: The Illusion of Destiny. Penguin Books (2007)
11. Varian, H.: Economic Aspects of Personal Privacy, UC, Berkeley, vol. 1 (1996)
12. Acquisti, A.: Is There a Cost to Privacy Breaches? In: International Conference on Information Systems 2006, vol. 1 (2006)
13. OECD, Economics of Malware: Security Decisions, Incentives and Externalities (2008)
14. Laudon, K.: Extensions to the Theory of Markets and Privacy: Mechanics of Pricing Information, vol. 1. Leonard N. Stern School of Business, New York University, New York (1997)
15. Horn, H.I., Hui, K.-L., Lee, T.S., Png, I.P.L.: The Value of Online Information Privacy: Evidence from the USA and Singapore, Marshall School of Business, University of Southern California Department of Information Systems, National University of Singapore, vol. 1 (2002)
16. Odlyzko, A.: Economics, Psychology, and Sociology of Security, Digital Technology Center, University of Minnesota, vol. 1
17. http://www.bbs-nordic.com/
18. Choudhary, B.: European E-Id Services: Future Trends and Nordic Experiences, FST Europe (2010)
19. http://www.ebay.com/
20. Resnick, P., Zeckhauser, R., Swanson, J., Lockwood, K.: The Value of Reputation on Ebay: A Controlled Experiment. Experimental Economics 9.2 (2005)
21. Melnik, M.I., Alm, J.: Does a Seller's Ecommerce Reputation Matter? Evidence from Ebay Auctions. Journal of Industrial Economics L (September 2002)
22. Mahadevan, B.: Business Models for Internet Based E-Commerce: An Anatomy. California Management Review 42.4 (2000)
23. Dellarocas, C.: Analyzing the Economic Efficiency of Ebay- Like Online Reputation Reporting Mechanisms. In: 3rd ACM Conference on Electronic Commerce, Tampa, USA, vol. 1 (2001)
24. http://www.identrust.com/
25. IdenTrust, The Identrust Rule Set: Providing Secure Identities While Protecting Privacy. IdenTrust, London (2007)
26. IdenTrust, Identity Authentication as a Critical Growth Strategy. IdenTrust, London (2007)

Profitable Investments Mitigating Privacy Risks

John Borking

Director Borking Consultancy, Wassenaar, Netherlands

Abstract. Risk control plays an important role at privacy protection. Article 17 (1) of the Directive 95/46/EC (DPD) requires that the controller must implement appropriate technical and organizational measures to protect personal data. ICT offers solutions in the shape of privacy protection for users, consumers and citizens. The application of ICT to protect privacy has become widely known under the name Privacy-Enhancing Technologies (PET or PETs). This chapter points out that a positive business case for the economic justification of investments in PETs is needed before a positive decision on the investment will be taken. The ROI and EPV calculation methods are useful tools for management assessing PET investments.

According to Article 23 of the DPD [1] a person who has suffered damage as a result of an unlawful processing operation or of any act incompatible with the national provisions adopted pursuant to DPD is entitled to receive compensation from the controller for the damage suffered. The controller may be exempted from this liability, in whole or in part, if he proves that he is not responsible for the event causing the damage.

The term risk is not defined in the DPD. The term risk is frequently used as if it is for everyone a univocal term. At closer consideration that is still but the question. Gratt, President of the American society or Risk Analysis (SRA) concluded after a two-years research that " a consensus was not being reached for the key definitions or risk and risk analysis". [2]

In this chapter as a definition of risk will be used: Risk = consequence *probability or (consequences_of_threat) * (likelihood_of _occurrence).[3]

A privacy threat analysis or a privacy impact analysis must be carried out examining the risks and documenting the results, before designing an information system that will be capable to protect personal data adequately against loss or against any form of unlawful processing. [4] A privacy risk analysis is mandatory according to the DPD as article 17 states that " (…) such measures shall ensure a level of security appropriate to the risks represented by the processing and the nature of the data to be protected."[1]

Schneier writes that " Threat Modeling is the first step in any security solution. It's a way to start making sense of the vulnerability landscape. What are the real threats against the system? If you don't know that, how do you know what kind of countermeasures to employ?" [5]

E. de Leeuw, S. Fischer-Hübner, L. Fritsch (Eds.): IDMAN 2010, IFIP AICT 343, pp. 59–72, 2010.
© IFIP International Federation for Information Processing 2010

1 The Privacy Risk Analysis

There are many ways determining privacy risks. The general approach for privacy risk analysis and subsequent requirements determination etc. is derived from a comparable domain: the risk assessment for information security in British Standards 7799, the Code of Practice for the Risk Analysis and Management Method, Information Security Handbook of the Central Computers and Telecommunications Agency (CCTA). [6] The pentagonal privacy threat analysis approaches threat identification and assessment of severity of consequences of such threats from five different perspectives:

- Privacy legislations, as defined in a certain country or country union: these regulations inherently list a number of privacy threats, if these regulations are not adhered to;
- Purpose of the system, which creates its own threats: because the user (private person) wants to achieve something, that person creates privacy threats;
- Solution adopted, which may or may not create threats of its own;
- Technology used: because of the way a certain system is implemented, certain threats may emanate which are not necessarily consequences of the intended purpose. Meanwhile, the technology will harbour some of the privacy enhancement measures;
- Situation in which the ultimate system will be used: which, although not necessarily creating threats of its own, may or may not aggravate (or alleviate) previously identified threats and hence may incur more demanding technological measures. This part is especially needed when a commercial off the shelf (COTS) product is going to be used in an unforeseen situation; the previous four types can be followed whether or not the system is a COTS or dedicated to a certain problem and environment. See figure 1.

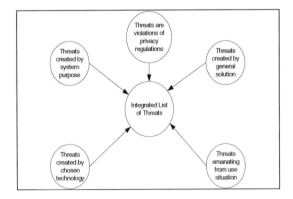

Fig. 1. Five-pronged approach to Privacy Threat Analysis [3]

Derived from the Directive 95/46/EC (DPD) the following risks or threats can be discerned:

- Secret possession of (control over) personal data files: the data subject and the authorities are unaware of the existence of the personal data and the control the controller of these data has;
- Secret processing of personal data: processing out of sight or knowledge of the data subject;
- Out of bounds processing by controller: processing of personal data that is not within the bounds stipulated in the personal data constraints or can be expected to be outside the scope and intention of the collection;
- Out of law processing: processing of personal data that is illegal, forbidden by national law (or is not explicitly allowed if it can be expected to be of dubious nature);
- Personal data deterioration: the personal data is in contradiction with the current situation, either caused by external changes or by incorrect or incomplete insertion, collection or insertion;
- Irresponsiveness to discontent: the controller does not respond, or incorrectly, incompletely or unduly late, to requests for correction or other implications to the personal data or the personal data constraints of a data subject; the controller thwarts communication; also: there is no authority with reprehension, correction, sanction or other influence on the controller to sustain the data subject's legal rights;
- Out of bounds processing by processor: the processor does not follow the personal data constraints as provided by the controller or violates the rules;
- Out of jurisdiction processing: the personal data are transferred to a controller which has no legal obligation to obey the personal data constraints or where legal obligations about privacy are less stringent than in the data subject's privacy regime;
- Personal data and personal data constraints violation: the controller and processor disobey the obligation to follow the personal data constraints concerning disclosure, retention, termination and safeguarding of correctness, including the obligation to take precautions against loss or mutilation of the personal data or the personal data constraints. [3]

2 Traditional Security Measures Not Sufficient

The requirements referred to in the DPD must be implemented efficiently in the organization in order to give proper support to the citizen's right to privacy with respect to personal data. It is therefore important to devise a proper system of general processing measures and procedures that should be present in order to protect company processes and in connection with specific protective measures for the processing of personal data. The restrictions that the organization of information systems can impose on the possibility that their users can comply with privacy legislation are evident. One simple example is where a system contains an inescapable 'date of birth' field, while analysis of the company's processes shows that recording the birth date of all persons included in the system is excessive. System design can just as easily ensure that users correctly observe the law. As a rule, privacy protection will constitute a supplementary system of measures and procedures in addition to the usual processing and security measures, but it should be assigned a significant place in management processes in order to implement and maintain a balanced processing policy for personal data.

When an organization is asked what it has done to protect privacy, it is apt to emphasize the personal data security measures it has in place. Although the use of safeguards to prevent unauthorized access to personal data is an important aspect of privacy protection, it is not sufficient in its own right. This is because such safeguards rarely involve the encryption of stored data; consequently, effective protection depends entirely on the security measures being correctly implemented and functioning properly.

It is therefore preferable to take technical measures that protect the individual's privacy at the point of data collection. Such measures may do away with the need to generate or record any personal data at all. Alternatively, they may minimize or even obviate the need to use or store identification data.

Given the basic legal requirements for privacy protection and the risks of privacy incidents, it will be apparent that, if technical provisions are to be deemed adequate, they must go beyond the implementation of traditional security measures.

3 Privacy Enhancing Technologies (PET)

ICT offers solutions in the shape of privacy protection for users, consumers and citizens. The application of ICT to protect privacy has become widely known under the name Privacy-Enhancing Technologies (PET or PETs). [6] PETs have been defined by the EU Commission as a coherent system of ICT measures that protects privacy by eliminating or reducing personal data or by preventing unnecessary and/or undesired processing of personal data; all without losing the functionality of the data system. [7][8]

PETs can guarantee data protection without making excessive demands on the processing of the data. By applying PETs and streamlining personal data processing, the organizations can continue to meet the high public expectations with respect to services and dealing with personal data.[9]

The basic driver to invest in PETs is their potential to avoid privacy incidents and so to reduce the risks and subsequently the damage caused by privacy breaches. In general terms a privacy incident can be defined as an event in which personal data are misused, because of the fact that personal data accompanied by a list with personal data constraints haven't been respected.

Privacy breaches may impact an organization in different ways. Tsiakis and Stephanides distinguish direct, short-term, and long-term economic consequences. [10] Direct consequences are the costs for repairing or changing systems, costs of stopping or slowing down production or processes, costs of legal action. Short term consequences comprise the loss of existing customers, contractual relations, and the loss of reputation. Companies may loose business because of privacy breaches, which harm their trust relationships with customers and other business relations. Safeguarding privacy has been identified as a major component of building trust.[11] Long term consequences include the loss of stock value and market value. An example of the latter is DoubleClick in 2000. After a serious violation of their existing privacy statement on their website and the lawsuit that was the result of this violation, their stock declined with 20%. [11] This also occurred with Choicepoint after their public announcement that they were hacked, and approximately 10 million data records were stolen. Their stock declined with 17% since the data breach. [6] The study on the economic benefits of privacy-enhancing technologies (PETs) from the EU Commission states that an obligation to notify privacy incidents would make risk assessment more accurate. [12]

3.1 Business Case for Pet Investments

Investments in (risk reducing) PET require insight into the costs and the quantitative and qualitative benefits. It is essential for the decision-making process concerning the investment for PET.[6]

The decision to spend money on privacy in any direction has to be financially justified. There is no point in implementing an expensive solution if a less expensive solution would offer the same risk reduction and because of that a better privacy protection. Beyond the legal compliance, it makes no sense to invest in a solution if its true costs are greater than the value it offers.

From the perspective of a business, privacy implies an investment to be measured in Euros saved as a result of reduced cost, or in additional revenues and profits from new activities that would not have occurred without an investment in privacy.

From the risk management literature a number of metrics have evolved to measure security risks, some of which apply to privacy risks as well. [13]

3.2 Annual Loss Expectancy

One of the most common measures for the assessing the risk of a harmful event is Annual Loss Expectancy, or ALE. ALE is the product of the expected yearly rate of occurrence of the event times the expected loss resulting from the occurrence. Other yardsticks here are SLE and ARO. SLE stands for the Single Loss Exposure; this is the true cost of a security incident. ARO means annual rate of occurrence; this is the
- frequency in which a risk happens on a yearly basis. The annual loss expectancy foreseen from all of an organization's operations would be the sum of the expected yearly losses that could result from multiple (privacy) threats. Determining adequate inputs to this ALE equation is however very difficult, due to lack of statistical data.

For example if a bank estimates the probability of a serious security incident at one of its subsidiaries during 2008 as one in a million and the direct and indirect cost of such incident as 150 million Euros, the ALE created by the risk of this security incident for 2008 will be € 15 million times 1/1,000,000 = € 150. Of course the actual costs of this risk will never be that of the ALE, but it will be either € 0 or €150 million. In most cases the situation will be less certain and the probability or cost may range between one in five hundred thousand and one in a million and the cost may vary between € 100 million and € 200 million. The ALE would then be between: (€100M or €200M) x (1/500,000,1/1,000,000) = €100 or €400. [14]

3.3 Return On Investment (ROI)

A metric that is quickly gaining in popularity is Return On Investments and specifically Return On Security Investments (ROSI). [15] Cardholm writes that: "Return on Investment (ROI) is a straightforward financial tool that measures the economic return of a project or investment. It is also known as return on capital employed. It measures the effectiveness of the investment by calculating the number of times the net benefits (benefits minus costs) recover the original investment. ROI has become one of the most popular metrics used to understand, evaluate, and compare the value of different investment options" [16]

The equation is: ROI = [(Savings from safeguards) + (profits from new ventures)] / costs of safeguards = [ALE (baseline) – ALE (with safeguards) + (profits from new ventures)] / (divided by) costs of safeguards. [13]

Hereunder follows an example. Suppose an organization decides to implement a Privacy Management System (PMS). The business case could be substantiated as follows:

If PMS were not implemented, the minimum annual costs for a company employing 1,000 staff to comply with privacy policies are estimated as follows:

1. Annual costs
Salary costs for Privacy Protection Officer (100% time allocation) Euro 100,000;
Management and secretarial salary costs Euro 40,000;
Costs for privacy audit Euro 30,000;
Security costs with respect to privacy compliance (excluding essential information security) Euro 20,000;
Report maintenance, regulations, settling registered people's rights, information, image and other damage, etc. Euro 20,000.
This leads to the total annual costs of Euro 210,000.

When comparing the situation where a PMS is used, the picture is as follows:

2. Development and implementation of PMS
For the acquisition of PMS has to be paid: Euro 150,000;
Consultancy for PMS implementation (60 days) costs Euro 80,000;
Start-up costs after implementation Euro 20,000.
The total one-off costs are Euro 250,000.

To these costs have to be added:
a. Annual costs PMS
b. PMS operational costs are Euro 30,000;
c. Maintenance costs are ± 15% of acquisition cost per annum: Euro 22,500;

d. Costs for privacy audit: Euro 10,000;

e. Salary costs for Privacy Protection Officer (50% time allocation) Euro 50,000;

In this situation the total costs are Euro 112,500.

The saving per annum compared with the situation when there wasn't an investment in PMS is Euro 210,000 - Euro 112,500 = Euro 97,500. Thus the extra investment costs for PMS would be already fully recovered after approx. two years and 2 months. [8]

3.4   Return On Security Investment (ROSI)

ROSI is a special application of ROI. The Return On Security Investments (ROSI) formula is the most well known ROSI calculation in the security industry. [6]

ROSI is an approach to look at the investment costs of security protection and the risk the investment removes. Assuming that the annual benefit of a security investment will be received throughout the lifetime of the investment, ROSI calculates the sum of the annual benefits over its cost. Benefits are calculated by adding expected cost savings to the new profit expected from new activities and sales.

Cardholm states that "it is basically a "savings" in Value-at-Risk; it comes by reducing the risk associated with losing some financial value". [16] Three core elements are determinative for the output calculation of the investment, namely: costs, turnovers and non-financial measurable elements. ROSI can be calculated using the equation below.

$$Rosi = \frac{(RiskExposure \cdot \%RiskMitigated) - SolutionCosts}{SolutionCost}$$

Fig. 2. ROSI Equation

The earlier discussed ALE can also be written as: Risk Exposure * %RiskMitigated or Risk mitigated because of the investment in security. [13]

The difficult parts in ROI method is determining ALE and SLE the risk-mitigating benefits of the security investment, since it is very difficult to know the true cost of a security incident. According to Sonnenreich, Albanese & Stout [15] there is very little known about those costs, because very few companies track those incidents.

Cardholm has a better approach with less uncertainty. His calculation is as follows:

ROSI = R − (R − E) + T,

or

ROSI = R − ALE, where ALE= (R - E) + T

The terms in Cardholm's equation can be described as:

  .·ALE: What we expect to lose in a year (Annual Loss Expectancy)

  .·R: The cost per year to recover from any number of incidents.

  .·E: These are the financial annual savings gained by mitigating any number of incidents through the introduction of the security solution.

  .·T: The annual cost of the security investment. [16]

3.5   ROI for Privacy Protection (ROIPI)

The ROI calculation methods can be applied also analyzing the return on investments that mitigates privacy risks, PET.

PET investments differ from "normal" ICT investments, since the investment may not directly improve the workflow, or does not make a process more efficient. The costs from PET are tangible and because of that are relatively easy to know. The benefits however are mostly intangible, because for example reputation improvement and a decreased risk for privacy incidents are not easy to quantify. However, these intangible benefits have the biggest value in a PET investment.

Luckily, the value of risk mitigated can be calculated using the method of Darwin (2007). The Darwin Calculator can be found at www.tech- 404.com/calculator.html.

The focus in this method will then be on the tangible benefits, the value of risk mitigated and the total costs, related to the PET investments. This method will be named: Return on Privacy Investments (ROIPI). How these figures will be calculated will be explained hereunder in more detail in the example of the Ixquick Europrise seal business case.

The formula is: ROIPI = {(TangibleBenefits +ValueOfRiskMitigated) – Total-Costs} divided (/) by the total costs

When the ROIPI gives a positive result, it means that the investment is beneficial for the company since the benefits outweigh the costs. Note that if the value of risk mitigated is positive this also has a positive influence on the ROIPI. The strong point of this formula is that it is not necessary to derive at an accurate estimate. The ROIPI only has to be precise enough to support the decision-making.

ROIPI assumes that the organization will fully comply with the law. This isn't often the fact. Violation of privacy, i.e. the illegal use of personal data, generates a lot of revenue and the chance that violation will lead to a prosecution is nil, due to the lack of resources of the National Data Protection Authorities.

3.6   Case Study: Ixquick

Ixquick is a meta searchmachine. The website of Ixquick be found at www.ixquick.com. Ixquick revenue model is the number of hits times the advertising benefits. The revenue is highly correlated to the search queries done through the site.

In 2003 and 2004, Internet traffic went down. In 2005, Internet traffic only went down with 5% and stabilized. In 2006 and 2007 the traffic increased again, due to the fact that Ixquick anonymized the IP addresses and search results in June 2006. Because of the anonymization, the traffic in 2006 and 2007 increased considerably. Due to the optimalization of the privacy protection of the users of the Ixquick meta search engine, triggered by the requirements for obtaining the EuroPrise privacy certificate (see www.european-privacy-seal.eu/about-europrise/fact-sheet) the number of visitors of the website increased again substantialy in 2008, thanks to the investment in the PET tool anonymization. With the increased traffic the revenue od Ixquick went up as well.

The reason of Ixquick for using PET was that it is a unique selling point; Ixquick became and is still the first fully anonymized meta search engine. Besides this reason the other driver was privacy risk minimalisation.

The investment costs for the PET tool were Euro 129.800, inclusive the extra investments needed for meeting the requirements of the EuroPrise certificate. The expenditure for the optimalized privacy protection amounted to € 37.000 for the technical and legal expertise. For press releases and communication costs announcing the Europrise privacy certificate award in July 2008 € 8.000 was spent. The mentioned costs were non-recurrent one-off expenses.

Moreover there are also recurring costs for the maintenance and the further development of the system amounting to € 16.500 per year. The total costs for the whole PET investment was: € 183.300.

The ROIPI equation can now be used for calculating whether Ixquick's privacy protection investment was the right decision of Ixquick's management.

ROIPI={(TangibleBenefits +ValueOfRiskMitigated) –TotalCosts} / (divided) by the total costs.

The total PET costs are Euro 183.300. The tangible benefits of using PET tools are the extra revenues in because of the increased data traffic. The directly tangible advantage for Ixquick due to the use of PET for the period of PET investments (2005-2008) is Euro 345.800. [6] To estimate the factor 'risk mitigated' the calculation tool of Darwin (2008) has been used. It will be assumed that in a privacy incident 10.000 records were stolen. Based on the daily users of the Ixquick search machine, the actual risk was much higher. The risk class of this data is of risk class II according to the guideline of the Dutch Data Protection Authority (CBP) [17] since the data consist of searches, these can consist of IP address, social security numbers and credit card numbers.

Based on the Darwin calculator (2008) the value of risk mitigated is Euro 1.050.300 on the 80% level (loss of 10.000 records) and the Dollar/Euro exchange rate in November 2008.

Using the values, the ROIPI equation produces as result:

TotalCosts= Euro183.300
TangibleBenefits= Euro 345,800
ValueofRiskMitigated= Euro 1.050.300
The intangible costs and benefits are appreciated as Euro 0 .
Thus ROIPI = {(345.800 + 1.050.300 + 0) – 183.300} / 183.300 =ROIPI = 6,6165 = approx. 662 % of the PET investment.

As this ROIPI value is very high, the conclusion is that the investment is very worthwhile. This number is also very high because of the value of risk mitigated. The ROIPI equation is especially preferable for SMEs because of its simplicity. This formula is a quick and reliable indicator whether the investment is worthwhile.

The intangible costs and benefits have been appreciated as zero euro, but if these intangible elements would be calculable, then the result would be even more favorable. However the ROIPI value is here significantly large enough to carry out the PET investment and to justify the investment from a business economy point of view.

Others advocate rightfully that organizations should discard the above equations and instead use discounted cash flow methods for investments that have different costs and benefits in different years. The theoretical flaw in ROI (and so in ROSI, ROIPI and related approaches) is that it processes financial figures irrespective of the dates that will be received or paid. The value of 1 euro today is not the same as of 1 euro in two years time. [13] The Discounted Cashflow methods (DCF) encompass two separate methods, the internal rate of return (IRR) and the Net Present Value (NPV). The allotted space for this chapter doesn't allow elaborating on the IRR method.

3.7 Net Present Value (NPV)

The Net Present Value (NPV) of a project or investment is defined as the sum of the present values of the annual cash flows minus the initial investment. The annual cash flows are the Net Benefits (revenues minus costs) generated from the investment during its lifetime. These cash flows are discounted or adjusted by incorporating the uncertainty and time value of money. NPV is one of the most robust financial evaluation tools to estimate the value of an investment. [16]

The calculation of NPV involves three simple yet nontrivial steps. The first step is to identify the size and timing of the expected future cash flows generated by the project or investment. The second step is to determine the discount rate or the estimated rate of return for the project. The third step is to calculate the NPV using the equations shown below:

NPV = initial investment + (Cash flow year 1 divided by $(1+r)1$) ... (Cash flow year 1 divided by $(1+r)n$)

Or:

$$NPV = \text{Initial investment (i)} + \sum_{t=1}^{t=\text{end of project}} \frac{(\text{Cash Flows at Year t})}{(1+r)^t}$$

The meaning of the terms is as follows:

·Initial investment (i): This is the investment made at the beginning of the project. The value is usually negative, since most projects involve an initial cash outflow. The initial investment can include hardware, software licensing fees, and start-up costs.

·Cash flow (cf_n): The net cash flow for each year of the project: Benefits minus Costs.

·Rate of Return (r): The rate of return is calculated by looking at comparable investment alternatives having similar risks. The rate of return is often referred to as the discount, interest, hurdle rate, or company cost of capital. Companies frequently use a standard rate for the project, as they approximate the risk of the project to be on average the risk of the company as a whole.

·Time (t): This is the number of years representing the lifetime of the project.

Experts are convinced that a company should invest in a project only if the NPV is greater than or equal to zero. If the NPV is less than zero, the project will not provide enough financial benefits to justify the investment, since there are alternative investments that will earn at least the rate of return of the investment. [16]

4 Economic Justification of Investments in Privacy Risk Reducing Pet

Within the context of the NPV method, the following data have to be collected:

1.The initial investment in privacy protection [I(p)], which encompasses cash outlays for Privacy Risk Analysis, process modeling, PET, implementation of PET, productivity loss, change management.

2.The yearly recurring cash flow, which contains all yearly financial effects of the proposal. This calculation bears on an analysis of expected cash flow patterns that would occur with and without the investment; it reflects a difference between two defined situations. The so-called 'without' situation will usually be the continuation of the current situation. This can for example be a situation with existing privacy protection in place, where the added value of PET is considered. The 'without' situation might also be a situation without any privacy protection. The definition of the 'without' situation depends on the starting position of the decision-maker.

Ribbers proposes to take into account the following cash flow components: Annual Loss Exposure (ALE), Reputation Recoverage Costs (RRC), Expected Revenue Accrual (ERA), Recurring Privacy Costs (RPC). [13]

ALE is the multiplied projected costs of a privacy incident and its annual rate of occurrence. Basically this encompasses revenue losses, legal claims, and productivity losses because of privacy breaches, repair costs and lost business.

RCC contain those expenses needed to restore the reputation of the company damaged by privacy breaches; examples are additional costs for PR and Marketing. Moreover if a privacy breaches affects the share price of the company (see ChoicePoint, Double Click), possibly breaches affects the share price of the company (see ChoicePoint, Double Click), banks and other financial institutions may require possibly additional financial guarantees.

ERA represents, on the positive side, possible marketing impacts on market share and revenue of publicized implementation of PET.

RPC contains the yearly (additional) privacy costs caused by the proposal; this will encompass needed privacy threat or impact analyses, audits, privacy officers etc.

As said, the analysis compares the project situation with the situation without the project. Basically this comes down to analyze the cash flow differences between the two situations. This can be done either by applying a factor RM (Risk Mitigated) to the situation without the investment or by subtracting the full-expected cash flow of the two situations from one another.

The RM factor for the applied privacy risk reducing/protection solution indicates what part of ALE and RRC has been compensated by the solution. Mitigated Risk is expressed as a reduction of the expected number of privacy breaches per year.

The resulting NPV of a privacy protection solution is consequently as follows:

$$\text{NPV} = - \text{I(p)} + \sum_{J=1}^{n} \{(\text{ALE} + \text{RRC})\,\text{RM} + \text{ERA} - \text{RPC}\} / (1+i)^{j}$$

Fig. 3. Privacy NPV equation [13]

4.1 The Case of the National Victim Tracking and Tracing System (VITTS)

The nation-wide implementation in the Netherlands of the Victim Tracking and Tracing System (ViTTS) is an important contribution to effective disaster management. The system provides regional medical officials with a concrete support to execute their tasks, through access to the required relevant contextual information,; it supports the allocation of injured persons to local and regional hospitals, and it provides the relevant competent authorities with necessary information. Moreover, municipalities will be better placed to execute mandatory registration procedures under the municipal disaster plan, and hospitals will be provided with timely information about the numbers of victims and the nature of their injuries. Due to the fact that sensitive personal medical information is processed about victims, the DPD requires optimal protection of such sensitive personal data. Privacy issues with respect to the health sector are particularly sensitive.

The EU PRIME ((Privacy and Identity Management for Europe) research team [6] has applied the NPV calculation approach in several case studies. One of the case studies is ViTTS. The following data have been collected from ViTTS.

The initial investment in privacy protection I(p) comprises the following components:

- System analysis and design, prototyping, test runs: Euro 15,000
- Privacy audit and Privacy risk assessment: Euro 50,000
- Smart Cards for on line authentication and encryption: Euro 25,000
- Implementation costs of PET measures: Euro 80,000

Total initial investment in reducing the risks of privacy incidents: Euro 170,000

Privacy breaches affecting the process of handling victims would have serious consequences and should be at all cost avoided. The privacy threat analysis showed that without privacy protection the VITTS system would undergo privacy breaches on a regular basis. The damage that would result from that can be estimated as follows.

The direct consequence of a breach (SLE – Single Loss Exposure) would be loss of reputation of the national government, possible wrong allocation of victims to hospitals with ineffective treatment and possibly deceases as a consequence. This may lead to significant legal claims. Claims of Euro 100,000 per case are not exceptional.

Such a breach would necessitate a nation-wide roll out of system adaptations: for which is needed two man-months per designated preventive health care safety region at Euro 100 per hour:

Total costs   Euro 347,000
Test and Trials to prove effectiveness of the system: Euro 80,000 per region:
Total cost   Euro 800,000
Training and education roll out: Euro 50,000
The total recovering costs (RCC) would amount to: Euro 1,197,000

The expected revenue accrual (ERA) can be estimated as follows. The most important reason for designated preventive health care safety regions to adopt the system is the built-in optimal privacy protection. So without privacy protection or with a much less rigid privacy protection there wouldn't have been developed such a system.

The estimated salary costs to replace the system by manual procedures would amount to 3 FTEs per region, which amounts to Euro 180,000 per region.

Nationwide this would result in a cost of: Euro 1,800,000

The total benefits of protecting privacy and reducing the risks of privacy incidents can be estimated at: Euro 2,277,000

(in this number legal claims are not included).

For the NPV calculation the following scenario is assumed: a time horizon of 6 years, a serious privacy breach every 2 years and a cost of capital of 5 %.

Applying the equation results into the following:

I(p): Euro 170,000;

Recurring cash flows:

- Costs avoided every two years: Euro 2,277,000
- Yearly recurring privacy costs: Euro 400,000
- Privacy costs in year 3 (no costs in year 6 given the assumption): Euro 25,000.

Under this assumption Ribbers' equation would lead to the following calculation:

NPV = - 170,000 + 2,277,000 (0.907029 +0.822702 +0.710681) – 25,000 (0.863838) – 400,000 (5.242137) = Euro + 3,268,368. [13]

This (positive) business case does not include possible legal claims.

The business case for the investment mitigating the risk of privacy incidents is positive. The ROI is 143,53%. Other scenarios lead to a positive business case as well. The privacy protection will even be profitable under the unrealistic assumption of a privacy breach only occurring once (and taking legal claims into account).

5 Conclusions

The ROI and NPV calculation methods are useful tools for management for assessing the (planned) investments in PET, reducing the risks of privacy incidents considerably.

ROI, ROSI and ROIPI provide useful insights. For a "quick and dirty" assessment of a PET investment ROIPI is useful especially for SMEs, like in the Ixquick business case. However ROIPI and other ROI methods are based on evaluating reductions in risks and do not take a time factor into account. The best approach would be to consider investments in PET as regular investments, characterized by cash flow patterns.

The Net Present Value approach is applied on the ViTTS case. This approach is effective in the context of assessing investments in PET, reducing privacy risks and enhancing privacy protection.

As many data are uncertain due to the lack of recording privacy incidents, scenarios have to be designed and assessed to give decision makers an understanding of the behavior of cost and benefit factors and their eventual effect on the business case outcome. Much more research on the economics of privacy protection has to be done. [12]

References

[1] Directive 95/46/EC, Official Journal L 281, 23/11/1995 P. 0031 – 0050
[2] Muller, E.R. (red.): Veiligheid, Studies over inhoud, organisatie en maatregelen, Alphen aan den Rijn (2004)
[3] van Blarkom, G.W., Borking, J.J., Olk, J.G.E.: Handbook of Privacy and Privacy-Enhancing Technologies. In: The Case of Intelligent Software Agents, Den Haag (2003), http://www.cbpweb.nl/downloadstechnologie/pisahandboek.pdf; cfr. Fritsch, L., Abie, H.: A Road Map to the Management of Privacy Risks in Information Systems, Oslo (2008)
[4] Flaherty, D.H.: Privacy Impact Assessments: An Essential Tool for Data Protection in Privacy Law & Policy Reporter, vol. 7(5) (October 2000)
[5] Schneier, B.: Threat Modeling and Risk Assessment. In: Baumler, H. (ed.) E-privacy, Datenschutz im Internet, Wiesbaden (2000)
[6] Borking, J.J.F.M.: Privacyrecht is Code, Over het gebruik van privacy Enhancing Technologies, Deventer (2010)
[7] Borking, J.: 'Der Identity Protector', Datenschutz und Datensicherheit 11 (1996); Hes, R., Borking, J.: Privacy-Enhancing Technologies: The Path to Anonymity, The Hague (1998)
[8] EU Commission, COM (2007) final
[9] Koorn, R., Van Gils, H., ter Hart, J., Overbeek, P., Tellegen, R., Borking, J.: Privacy Enhancing Technologies, Witboek voor Beslissers, Ministerie van Binnenlandse Zaken en Koninkrijksrelaties Den Haag (2004)
[10] Tsiakis, T., Stephanides, G.: The economic approach of information security. Computers & Security 24 (2005)
[11] Chapman, S., Dhillon, G.S.: Privacy and the internet: the case of DoubleClick, Inc. – Social Responsibility in the Information Age: Issues and Responsibilities. Fort Lauderdale-Davie (2002)
[12] Final report to the European Commission DG Justice, Freedom and Security, Study on the economic benefits of privacy-enhancing technologies (PETs), Brussels (2010)
[13] Fairchild, A., Ribbers, P.: Privacy-Enhancing Identity Management in Business. In: Camenish, J., Leenes, R., Sommer, D. (eds.) Privacy and Identity Management for Europe, Brussels (2008)
[14] Blakley, B., McDermott, E., Geer, D.: Information management is Information Risk Management. In: Proceeding NSPW 2001, Cloudcroft, New Mexico (2002)
[15] Sonnenreich, W., Albanese, J., Stout, B.: Return on Security Investment (ROSI) – A Practical Approach. Journal of Research and Practice in Information Technology 38(1) (February 2006)
[16] Cardholm, L.: Adding Value to business performance through cost benefit analyses of information security management, Gävle (2006)
[17] van Blarkom, G.W., Borking, J.J.: Beveiliging van Persoonsgegevens, Achtergrond en-Verkenningen 23, Den Haag 2001 Privacy Rights Clearinghouse: A Chronology of Data Breaches (2007), http://www.privacyrights.org/ar/ChronDataBreaches.htm#CP

A Security Analysis of OpenID

Bart van Delft[1] and Martijn Oostdijk[2]

[1] Comp. Sci. Dept., Radboud Univ., P.O. Box 9010, 6500 GL,
Nijmegen, The Netherlands
`b.vandelft@student.ru.nl`
[2] Novay, P.O. Box 589, 7500 AN, Enschede, The Netherlands
`martijn.oostdijk@novay.nl`

Abstract. OpenID, a standard for Web single sign-on, has been gaining popularity both with Identity Providers, Relying Parties, and users. This paper collects the security issues in OpenID found by others, occasionally extended by the authors, and presents them in a uniform way. It attempts to combine the shattered knowledge into a clear overview. The aim of this paper is to raise awareness about security issues surrounding OpenID and similar standards and help shape opinions on what (not) to expect from OpenID when deployed in a not-so-friendly context.

1 Introduction

In 2005 Brad Fitzpatrick developed the first version of the OpenID protocol. Initially intended to save users the effort of going through a registration process on multiple social (blogging) websites they wanted to join, the protocol has by now become a very popular single sign-on method on a large number of high profile websites (JanRain claims over 30,000 OpenID enabled websites in January 2009 [5]). In fact, given an average user on the Internet, chances are high that he or she already owns a so-called 'OpenID enabled login', since Google, Yahoo, Facebook, AOL and Windows Live accounts all support OpenID.

The latest version of the OpenID Authentication specification, version 2.0 [20], was released in December 2007[1]. The new version mainly enabled more flexibility and support for the possible identities to use, improved some security aspects and enabled the usage of extensions for attribute exchange.

This paper studies the security aspects of the OpenID 2.0 specification and its implementations. Information in this area has been around for some time. During the BlackHat USA conference in 2007, Eugene and Vlad Tsyrklevich listed a number of potential issues [22], and a similar collection can be found on [15]. Several singular findings have been reported on blogs and wikis as well, but this information is scattered and the possible impact is difficult to assess. By collecting these issues and looking at the underlying mechanisms of reported

---

[1] The original version written by Brad Fitzpatrick had no version number but is commonly referred to as OpenID 1.0. OpenID 2.0 is based on OpenID 1.1, which is a revised version of the original version from Fitzpatrick.

E. de Leeuw, S. Fischer-Hübner, L. Fritsch (Eds.): IDMAN 2010, IFIP AICT 343, pp. 73–84, 2010.

attacks, this paper contributes to the existing literature by trying to pinpoint the root causes and possible solutions of OpenID security issues.

In relation to this paper, the original goal of OpenID should be kept in mind. OpenID was meant for authentication to 'simple' websites, blogs and the like. It was not intended for high-trust applications, such as e-banking. The requirement to ensure that claims about a user are actually correct, the so-called *level of assurance*, was low.

The OpenID protocol is not unique in its goals, nor in its methods. Several other web single sign-on specifications have been drafted with roughly the same targets in mind, the *SAML Web Browser Single Sign On* profile probably being the most notable [7]. The main differences between SAML and OpenID is that SAML requires the web applications involved to know each other beforehand, and that it is part of a far larger specification. The SAML specification was drafted by industrial companies whereas OpenID is a community-driven project. Other specifications in (roughly) the same category include OAuth [17] and WS-Trust [11], and Information Card [16].

1.1   OpenID from the User's Perspective

To explain the OpenID concepts this section presents an example scenario from the user's perspective. The example introduces terminology used throughout the remainder of this paper.

A *User* is going to register himself at the web application springnote.com (the *Relying Party, RP*). Instead of filling out yet another registration form he provides the RP a URL that represents his identity, say www.johndoe.com (the *Identity URL* or *claimed identifier*). At this URL the RP can *discover* how it should verify the user's ownership of this URL. In this example the RP discovers that the owner of this URL should be able to log on at openid.yahoo.com (the *OpenID Provider, OP*) with username jdoe.

The RP redirects the user to the OP where he is asked to enter the password for username jdoe. After authentication of this *local identity* the user is asked whether he indeed wants to use his identity on *.springnote.com (the *realm*) and send along the *attributes* as requested by the RP (such as the user's full name and email address). If confirmed the user is redirected back to the RP.

Using a direct connection the RP ensures that the local identity is indeed authenticated by the OP. Assuming that no one except the owner can alter the content of www.johndoe.com, springnote is assured that this user is in fact the owner of this URL. The RP can now create a local account on its web application for this identity or, in the case of a returning user, log him in using this identity.

1.2   OpenID from a Technical Perspective

In order to understand all of the security issues described in Section 2, some knowledge of the OpenID 2.0 specification [19] is required. This section gives a global introduction to the protocol. Figure 1 gives a schematic overview of the protocol.

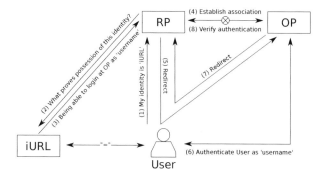

Fig. 1. Schematic overview of the protocol. Note that there is an exclusive OR-relation between step (4) and step (8).

Discovering the User's Identity. The RP fetches the Identity URL as specified by the user in order to discover his OP. In the current version there can be either a static link stating the OP and the local identity, or an XRDS-document can be used enabling the possibility of specifying different OPs for multiple protocols. In the latter case Yadis[2] is used to discover the OP and protocol version to use.

Establishing an Association. An *association* is used to ensure that no one but the OP has authenticated the user's local identity. Instead of using associations the RP could also choose to skip this step and validate an identity assertion at the end of the protocol run.

An association is established between the RP and the OP and consists of an *association_handle*, which is a unique name for this association, and a *MAC key* (Message Authentication Code) for signing messages. There are two methods to establish an association; one using Diffie-Hellman (DH) key exchange [4], and one requiring a secure channel (e.g. SSL).

Redirecting to the OP. After the discovery of the OP and the optional setup of an association, the RP forwards the user via a web redirect to the OP. This request again contains a number of parameters, most notable the claimed identity, the association handle (if applicable), the domain of the RP that needs to be allowed (the *realm*) and a URL at the RP where the user agent should be redirected after authentication (`return_to`).

Redirecting to the RP. When the OP has authenticated the user's local identity and the user has allowed his identity to be used on the specified realm, the

---

[2] The Yadis protocol was developed by (roughly) the same community as OpenID, but is in its functionality not linked to it. Yadis used to be the original name for OpenID, being an acronym for "Yet Another Distributed Identity System".

OP redirects the user to the RP with a number of parameters. These include the association handle (if applicable), a server-time based nonce to prevent replay attacks and a signature over the values of a number of these parameters, including the parameters mentioned here. If an association was established this signature is based on the MAC key and signing algorithm specified in that association.

Verifying the Response. If no association had been established the RP still has to ensure the response was indeed generated by the OP. The RP sends the parameters received directly to the OP and the OP responds with, amongst others, an is_valid parameter stating whether the signature was his.

2   A Classification of Security Issues

This section categorises security issues found into four categories. The categories represent different features of the goal that OpenID is trying to achieve, of typical implementation practice, of the OpenID specification, and of the underlying infrastructure of the Web.

Similar collections and discussions can be found in [8–10, 12, 14, 22].

Single Sign On. The goal that OpenID is trying to achieve is usually referred to as Single Sign On (SSO) for the Web. The central idea behind SSO is that once a user has authenticated to an OP, he or she does not have to do so again. Within the context of typical OpenID provider implementations this also means that once a user has granted a permanent approval for a RP, this request for approval is not shown again.

Open to anyone. An important feature of OpenID is that a user is able to choose his or her own Identity (URL), OP, and RPs. In principle, anyone can join and implement an OP or start accepting OpenID transactions as a RP.

OpenID-specific issues. Some specific choices made in the OpenID specification, or lack thereof, lead to differences and possible weaknesses in implementations.

Use of Web standards. Web-redirects are used to send the user from the RP to the OP and back again. While this makes light-weight requirements for OP, RP, and user, it also means that OpenID inherits weaknesses present in this redirection mechanism.

This distinction makes clear that not all vulnerabilities found threaten OpenID alone. Some are also applicable to other standards. The issues corresponding to these categories are listed in the sections below. Some of the issues fall into multiple categories.

2.1   The Single Sign on Concept

Adversaries will Focus on OPs. A user uses the same OP to log in to multiple RPs. If an attacker is able to steal these credentials he obtains access to multiple

RPs including the data the user has stored there. The credentials stored at an OP become more valuable with the popularity of the OpenID standard.

On the other hand, once OpenID becomes the de facto standard for Web SSO, OPs are able to focus solely on the protection of its users data and implementation can be hardened.

When registering on a non-OpenID enabled website, a valid email address is often required. If a user forgets his password, this password or a reset option can be sent to his email address. Thus if an attacker successfully hacks a large email provider, e.g. Live mail, his gain will be roughly the same. A main difference is that in the OpenID scenario an attacker will not need to change the user's password, making the actions harder to detect.

Spying OPs. As a result of always using the same OP to log in, the OP has the possibility to log every transaction with every RP the user visits. It knows the frequency, what times of the day etc. [22]. The OP's effort is just the logging of every transaction. Data mining tools are widely available for handling the resulting data, making this a feasible attack.

Compared with an OpenID-less setting, only the user's web browser is in a comparable position. Consider the Google Chrome web browser that sends every URL a user visits to the Google datacenters where these are (anonymously?) processed for improvement of the browser and other Google products. The concept of a (service-)provider you use for visiting other website collecting data on you is thus not new.

Cross-Site Scripting. When a user is logged in to his OP and has permanently granted permission for a RP, the user will not be prompted with either the OP's login screen nor with the request for identifying himself to this specific RP. This allows for an extension of existing cross-site scripting attacks. An attacker could place a hidden frame on a website loading the OpenID-login from the targeted RP, in that manner logging the visitor in to that RP without this victim being aware. The attacker can now perform cross-site request forgery (XSRF) attacks such as performing actions on the RP in that user's name [22].

As a result, "logging out when finished" as is commonly advised, no longer guarantees protection against XSRF attacks. XSRF protection needs to be in place at the RP, as will be described in Section 3.3.

A different attack in this category is *clickjacking* [6] where stylesheet features are abused to make a user think he clicks a link (on a website controlled by the attacker) while in fact clicking a translucent button or link above it. In this manner some interaction can be accounted for.

Session Swapping. In this attack an adversary tricks the user into visiting a replica page the user assumes to be a certain RP. The website however abuses the no-interaction log on to automatically log the user on to the real RP under an account controlled by the attacker. Being accustomed to the SSO-principle, the user will be assuming he was signed on to his own account [10]. In order to reduce the risk of the user noticing the session swap the attacker should be aware of personal information of the user on the RP, such as username, personal background image etcetera.

If successful, the potential gain of an attacker would be search phrases or credit card information entered by the user on the RP in the assumption that this is his own account. Being the real owner of the account, the attacker can later retrieve this information by logging on to the RP. A large amount of luck is however required.

2.2   Open to Anyone

The Port-Scanning RP. At the beginning of the protocol the RP fetches the Identifier URL as specified by the user. Since the user is free in choosing the value of this URL, an adversary could enter URLs such as http://www. example.com:21, hereby abusing the RP as a (proxied) port-scanner. It might, depending on the RP's configuration, even be possible to scan internal locations such as 192.168.1.45:3654 [22].

Port-scanning in itself is not much of a threat, but having the possibility to scan addresses *within* the local network of the RP and the fact that this scanning easily can be automated makes it a possibly useful component in a targeted attack.

RP Getting Lost in Discovery. This attack abuses the fact that the RP has to connect to the Identifier URL as provided by the user. A malicious user could use large or endless files as Identifier URLs in an attempt to perform a DoS (Denial of Service attack) on the RP [22]. He does however first have to find an RP vulnerable to this attack, i.e. an RP that does not halt after hitting a limit during the fetching of a URL. Since it is trivial to mount such an attack, it is highly likely someone will try.

2.3   OpenID-Specific Issues

Diffie-Hellman / Man in the Middle Attack. As described in Section 1.2, Diffie-Hellman key exchange may be used to establish an association and send the corresponding MAC key from the OP to the RP. DH key exchange is vulnerable to a *Man in the Middle* (MitM) attack, where an attacker is acting as the OP to the RP and as the RP to the OP. This results in the attacker being able to change all the data being send from the OP to the RP, without the RP noticing that the signature is incorrect. Depending on the location of this Man in the Middle, he could either log in to one RP as being any user, or log in as any user from one OP to any RP [22].

In order to perform a MitM attack, the attacker either needs to have something in between the two parties (the RP and the OP) such as a router functioning as a proxy, or perform a DNS spoofing attack.

As long as RPs using OpenID only require low-level security (e.g. blogs, comment-systems) the effort of performing a MitM will probably outrank the gain. However, when large web shops or online payment companies start accepting OpenID intensively, a MitM attack becomes more tempting for an attacker.

Association Poisoning. In this attack an attacker sniffs the name of an association (the association handle) for a specific RP / OP communication. He then logs in to the RP using his own OP. Since the OP gets to choose the handle, the attacker chooses the exact same handle he just sniffed, making a vulnerable RP *overwrite* the original MAC key with the one specified by the attacker. The attacker may now, for a limited amount of time (if or until the real OP overwrites the handle again), modify the attributes sent from the OP to the RP, using his own signature to sign. If the attacker does not change these messages, the RP will think that the message from the OP are incorrectly signed and thus rejected [2].

To alter the data sent from the OP to the RP, the attacker has (as in the MitM attack) to install a node in between the two parties. Otherwise the only result will be that the messages from the original OP will be rejected by the RP. A quick review on *DotNetOpenId* and *JanRain's OpenID Ruby library* by [2] and a review on *openid-php* by the authors show that this attack cannot be performed against these commonly used libraries.

OpenID Recycling. A user may change from OP over time, leaving his local identity to be taken by a new user. If his OP is at the same time the supplier of his Identity URL (which is the case if e.g. username.myid.net or the Google / Yahoo! etc. buttons are directly used) this means that not only his local identity, but also his Identity URL are now owned by the new user. Without precautions the new user could log in to an RP and find the data of the previous owner of that Identity URL, since the RP cannot differentiate between them. The new owner does not have to be an adversary for this situation to arise.

The OpenID 2.0 Specification does provide a recommended solution to this problem in the form of *fragments* (section 11.15.1 in the specification). However because OPs are not *required* to adopt this solution, identity recycling issues might still occur.

2.4   Use of Web Standards

Phishing. In a phishing attack a user is tempted to visit a website impersonating the login-screen of the user's OP. If he fails to notice that this is not the official website of the OP and enters his credentials, the attacker is able to copy these credentials [14] [21].

Previous phishing attacks often required the user to click a suspiciously formatted link, but the addition of OpenID's redirection setup makes it possible to create a less questionable attack. An RP controlled by an adversary could simply redirect users to a phishing OP instead of to their real OP, without the users noticing anything different from a regular login. The risk of being phished therefore increases with the introduction of OpenID.

Realm Spoofing. This attack [14] assumes the existence of a RP having an XSS- or other vulnerability enabling forwarding to other websites, e.g. `http://www.example.com?goto=http://evil.com`. An attacker creates a website imitating this RP and if the user tries to log in using OpenID the attacker tells the OP that his realm is the one of the official RP and in the return-to URL (Section 1.2) abuses the forward possibility that will redirect the user back to his website.

If successful, both the OP and the user will believe that the attributes are send to the official RP, but these are, although the OP compared the realm and the return-to URL correctly, in fact redirected to the imitating RP of the attacker.

To summarise the results of this section, Table 1 provides an overview of the security issues. The rightmost two columns of the table gives qualitative risk estimates for two scenarios: one in which OpenID is used for services with level of assurance (LOA, see [18]) equal to 1, and one in which OpenID is used for services with a higher LOA. The risk estimates are based on the combination of effort required for the specific attack, and the gain an attacker may receive from a successful attempt. The main difference between the two scenarios is based on the assumption that services with a higher LOA imply more potential gain for the attacker, increasing the likeliness that a specific vulnerability will be abused.

As may be derived from this table, the average risk in a LOA of 1 is roughly moderate, while the average risk for services with a higher LOA would be high when OpenID is deployed in that scenario.

Table 1. An overview of the security issues listed in this paper. L = Low, M = Moderate, H = High risk.

Category	Vulnerability	Threat	LOA = 1	LOA > 1
Single Sign On	Always use same OPs	Attacks focus on them	L	M
		OP tracks its users	M	M
	No-interaction log in	Cross-site scripting	H	H
		Session Swapping	L	M
Being Open	Specify any Identity URL	Port-scanning RP	M	M
		RP lost in discovery	H	H
OpenID-specific	Usage of Diffie-Hellman	MitM attack	L	H
	Mild specification	Association poisoning	M	H
		OpenID recycling	-	-
Use of Web standards	RP redirects user to OP	Phishing	H	H
	User is in a browser	Clickjacking	M	H
		Realm spoofing	-	-

3 An Overview of Solutions

This section lists possible directions for solutions to the issues described in Section 2. The solutions are grouped into a number of categories to show how they may be applied. Figure 2 gives an overview.

3.1 Trust Frameworks

Most of the problems arising from the 'Open' part of OpenID can be solved by becoming more closed, e.g. via the usage of a trust framework between Identities, OPs and RPs. If these parties get whitelisted all attacks requiring the attacker to control one or more of these parties can be prevented. As a consequence it will no longer be possible to add an OpenID-login to every potential RP, neither will the end-users be able to use any Identifier or OP of their liking.

As an example the Federal Identity, Credential and Access Management (ICAM) committee of America recently profiled OpenID for Level of Assurance 1 [18] transactions with the Federal government [13]. In this profile a whitelist at the ICAM website specifies the OPs that RPs can trust during the authentication process.

3.2 Anti-phishing Techniques

There are two main directions in preventing phishing attempts. First the OP can add personalisation elements such as a personal icon to its login-pages. These icons are cookie-based and will therefore only work when the user visits the OP from a single web browser. Secondly additional client-side software (notably add-ons for web browsers) can be installed to assist the user in noticing potential phishing attacks. This includes tools for helping users to check certificates and domain addresses (such as the address bar highlighting, default in several browsers[3]) and OpenID specific add-ons, such as VeriSign's SeatBelt[4], Sxipper[5] and Microsoft's Identity Selector[6]. A special and creative solution is BeamAuth, suggested by Adida et al. [1] making use of bookmarks and not requiring the user to install additional software.

3.3 Preventing Cross-Site Scripting Attacks

Several measures can be taken by RPs and OPs to counter cross-site scripting attacks. Using JavaScript to ensure the RP or OP is not loaded in a (hidden) frame will prevent several of them. Another option for both RPs and OPs is to require a *reduced sign on*, i.e. session-information is not used but the user has to (re-)authenticate himself to the OP for every (or: for this specific) RP.

---

[3] This is a default feature of both Internet Explorer and Chrome, and can be installed to Mozilla Firefox as the Locationbar[2] add-on.

[4] https://pip.verisignlabs.com/seatbelt.do

[5] http://www.sxipper.com

[6] http://self-issued.info/?p=235

Since cross-site scripting is no new threat, existing solutions can be used as well. It is for instance recommended to add *nonces* to every user-interaction on the application of the RP. This will prevent an attacker from performing automatic actions with the identity of another user.

3.4 Specification Adaptations

A number of problems can be solved or mitigated by addressing them in the OpenID 2.0 specification [19]. The matters of abusing a RP as a port-scanner or performing a DoS on them by presenting a maliciously chosen Identifier URL (Section 2.2) could be addressed by requiring some additional standardisation of the Identifier URL. This could include the refusal of URLs containing port-numbers and local ip-addresses.

A second requirement could be the RP having to set a nonce in the User-Agent initiating the protocol to check whether this nonce still exists at the end of the protocol session, in that way recognizing a Session Swapping attempt (Section 2.1).

A last way of addressing some of the issues is by enforcing secure choices over convenient choices in the OpenID specification. This can be done by changing occurrences of the key words MAY and SHOULD by MUST (as specified in [3]). Examples of this solution are: enforcing the use of HTTPS for communication between OP and RP, and enforcing the use of fragments to prevent identity recycling.

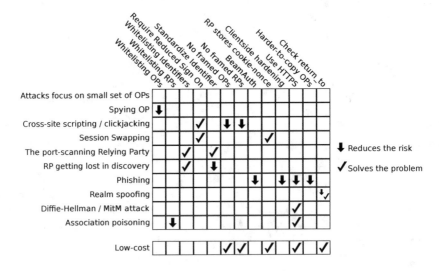

	Whitelisting OPs	Whitelisting RPs	Whitelisting Identifiers	Require Reduced Sign On	Standardize Identifier	No framed OPs	No framed RPs	RP stores cookie-nonce	Clientside hardening	Harder-to-copy OPs	Use HTTPS	Check return_to
Attacks focus on small set of OPs												
Spying OP	↓											
Cross-site scripting / clickjacking				✓		↓	↓					
Session Swapping				✓					✓			
The port-scanning Relying Party			✓		✓							
RP getting lost in discovery			✓			↓						
Phishing									↓	↓	↓	↓
Realm spoofing												↓✓
Diffie-Hellman / MitM attack											✓	
Association poisoning				↓							✓	
Low-cost						✓	✓		✓		✓	✓

↓ Reduces the risk

✓ Solves the problem

Fig. 2. An overview on which solutions are solving what problems. Low-cost refers to the costs of applying this solution in terms of money, user experience and restriction it places on RPs and OPs (i.e. whitelisting).

4 Conclusions and Future Research

In this paper a set of security issues concerning OpenID are discussed, as well as possible solutions to these issues. Applying the low-cost solutions already solves about a third of the issues, making the application of these solutions a strong recommendation to every party using OpenID.

Taking the security issues into account that remain after the application of these low-cost solutions, one can conclude that OpenID was intended and should only be used in applications where a LOA [18] no higher than 1 is required. This level implies that the specification is only to be used in situations where no negative consequences result from erroneous authentication.

Future research could include an investigation to the elements of the OpenID specification that need to be altered in order to make it applicable for applications with a LOA greater than 1 as well. In the context of future internet, the specification would also benefit from becoming even more dynamic and allow for automated negotiations between applications with different LOA levels. Available information suggests that this is most easily achieved when a trust framework is added. Figure 2 shows that when both the whitelisting and the low-cost solutions are applied almost all security issues are solved, except for the possibly inescapable phishing problem and value raise of credentials at OPs.

Adding a framework of trust to OpenID lifts it to a different level and solves many of the issues. Doing so moves it into the direction of competing standards such as SAML, WS-Trust, and Information Card. However, such a move likely changes the standard in character, and is a move away from what it was initially intended for: Web SSO where anybody can select their OP and set of RPs of choice. The challenge thus lies in finding a trust model that makes OpenID secure, yet retains OpenID's open and dynamic character.

Acknowledgments. The research described in this paper was carried out in the context of the *cidSafe* project (http://cidsafe.novay.nl) which is part of the *Service Innovation & ICT* programme (http://www.si-i.nl).

References

1. Adida, B.: BeamAuth: Two-Factor Web Authentication with a Bookmark. In: ACM Conference on Computer and Communications Security, pp. 48–57 (2007)
2. Arnott, A.: OpenID Association Spoofing. blog.nerbank.net (March 2009), http://blog.nerdbank.net/2009/03/openid-association-poisoning.html
3. Bradner, S.: Key words for use in RFCs to Indicate Requirement Levels. RFC 2119 (1997)
4. Diffie, W., Hellman, M.E.: New directions in Cryptography. IEEE Transactions on Information Theory IT-22, 644–654 (1976)
5. Drebes, L.: Relying Party Stats as of Jan 1st, 2009. JanRain Blog (January 2009), http://blog.janrain.com/2009/01/relying-party-stats-as-of-jan-1st-2008.html
6. Hansen, R., Grossman, J.: Clickjacking (September 2008), http://www.sectheory.com/clickjacking.htm

7. Hughes, J., Cantor, S., Hodges, J., Hirsch, F., Mishra, P., Philpott, R., Maler, E.: Profiles for the OASIS Securit Assertion Markup Language (SAML) V2.0 (March 2005), http://docs.oasis-open.org/security/saml/v2.0/

8. Oh, H.-K., Jin, S.-H.: The security limitations of SSO in OpenID. In: 2008 10th International Conference on Advanced Communication Technology, Gangwon-Do, South Korea, Piscataway, NJ, USA, February 17-20, pp. 1608–1611. IEEE, Los Alamitos (2008)

9. Jain, A., Hodges, J.: Openid review (November 2009), https://sites.google.com/site/openidreview/

10. Jain, A., Nash, A., Hodges, J.: OpenID Security Issues. Presentation PayPal Information Risk Management (November 2009)

11. Lawrence, K., Kaer, C.: WS-Trust 1.4 OASIS Editor Draft (February 2008), http://docs.oasis-open.org/ws-sx/ws-trust/200802/ws-trust-1.4-ed-01.html

12. Lindholm, A.: Security Evaluation of the OpenID Protocol. Master's thesis, Sveriges Största Tekniska Universitet, Sweden (2009)

13. McBride, T., Silver, D., Tebo, M., Louden, C., Bradley, J.: Federal Identity, Credentialing, and Access Management - OpenID 2.0 Profile. Release Candidate 1.0.1 (November 2009), http://www.idmanagement.gov/documents/ICAM_OpenID20Profile.pdf

14. Messina, C.: OpenID Phising Brainstorm (December 2008), http://wiki.openid.net, http://wiki.openid.net/OpenID_Phishing_Brainstorm

15. Anonymous (most likely Ashish Jain and Jeff Hodges) (2009), https://sites.google.com/site/openidreview/

16. Nanda, A.: Identity Selector Interoperability Profile V1.0 (2007)

17. oauth.net. OAuth Core 1.0 Revision A (June 2009), http://oauth.net/core/1.0a/

18. Office of Management and Budget (OMB). E-Authentication Guidance for Federal Agencies, Memorandum M-04-04 (December 2003), http://www.whitehouse.gov/omb/memoranda/fy04/m04-04.pdf

19. openid.net. OpenID Authentication 2.0 - Final (December 2007), http://openid.net/specs/openid-authentication-2_0.html

20. Recordon, D., Reed, D.: OpenID 2.0: A platform for User-Centric Identity Management. In: Conference on Computer and Communications Security Proceedings of the Second ACM Workshop on Digital Identity Management, Alexandria, Verginia, USA, pp. 11–16 (2006)

21. Tom, A., Arnott, A.: OpenID Security Best Practices. openid.net (July 2009), http://wiki.openid.net/OpenID-Security-Best-Practices

22. Tsyrklevich, E., Tsyrklevich, V.: Single Sign-On for the Internet: A Security Story. In: BlackHat USA (2007)

Personal Federation Control with the Identity Dashboard

Jonathan Scudder[1] and Audun Jøsang[2]

[1] Department of Informatics, University of Oslo, Norway
jonathas@ifi.uio.no
[2] UniK Graduate Center, University of Oslo, Norway
josang@unik.no

Abstract. Current federated identity management solutions for open networks do not solve the scalability problems for users. In some cases, federation might even increase the identity management complexity that users need to handle. Solutions should empower users to actively participate in making decisions about their identity, but this is far from the current situation. This paper proposes the *Identity Dashboard* as a user-centric control component, providing users with tools they need to effectively partake in managing their own identities.

Keywords: Identity management, federation, SSO, single sign on, usability, security, authentication, SAML, privacy, privacy enhancing technologies.

1 Introduction

Digital identities represent who we are when engaging in online activities and transactions. The rapid growth in the number of online services leads to an increasing number of different identities that each user needs to manage. At the same time, there is a proliferation of sensitive information on the Internet as the volume of personal details required by systems and sites is increasing.

Identity federation reduces this burden to a certain degree by addressing the transport of identity assertions [1] between service providers and identity providers. Identity federation is strictly standards-based to allow interoperability between autonomous parties. These standards describe authentication-related messages and the ways in which they are passed between federated entities in order to allow a relying party to trust that a user has identified themselves to an asserting party. The two most widespread standards are SAML [1] and WS-Federation [2]. SAML 2.0 is a convergence of the Liberty ID-FF [3], Internet2 Shibboleth [4], and earlier SAML standards.

Other more recent developments include "user-centric" approaches to federation, such as Cardspace [12] and Higgins [13]. User-centric approaches have a different paradigm for handling user attributes which utilize client-based storage and authorization [14,15]. In contrast to network-based federations where the personal identity information is not stored locally, user-centric approaches

E. de Leeuw, S. Fischer-Hübner, L. Fritsch (Eds.): IDMAN 2010, IFIP AICT 343, pp. 85–99, 2010.

are not subject to concerns about who is in control of the data, which is the main motivation for this paper.

Identity federation opens the door to a win-win situation whereby the user experience is simpler, no longer requiring the user to log on to accounts individually, and at the same time more secure since user credentials can be better protected. For example, if a user only needs one password where they previously needed 10 passwords, then the new password can conceivably be longer, and changed more often without overtaxing the user. Due to the degree of trust involved in creating identity federations, legal and organisational requirements are also paramount, and are partially addressed by the prevailing standards.

A major challenge to federation is realising user-control. A user should ideally know which services they can access, and which attributes are being shared between identity providers and service providers. This is difficult to achieve in practice since the required information is not necessarily collected at a single point. An identity provider may know which attributes it is willing to make available to service providers, but only a subset of these may be requested by the service provider, and this may be controlled dynamically at runtime.

Another challenge to federation is that the degree of trust required does not foster truly large-scale federations. Thus the dream of a single sign-on where identity is authenticated only once for virtually all systems will not likely be achieved with the current frameworks alone. This leads to a future where users will have relationships to an increasing number of federations. The emergence of "super federations" which connect individual federations in inter-trust relationships leads to a less clear picture of how the user's identity is handled, and where identity attributes are being shared.

The development of identity federation technologies was inspired by the need to improve the user experience when accessing online services. Ironically, the technology-centric approach followed is now causing new usability problems that the SAML 2.0 and WS-Federation specifications do not account for.

This paper examines the need for user control in a SAML 2.0 federated environment, and proposes requirements for a new component called the Identity Dashboard in order to provide the user with a central point of contact through which they can effectively manage their federated identities. The Identity Dashboard is envisaged realised through extensions to the OASIS SAML 2.0 standard based on the requirements discovered.

Note that privacy *policies* have been explored elsewhere [11,5,6]. The Identity Dashboard addresses the problem of monitoring; having expressed the wish that an attribute should not be shared or used as an identifier, for example, has limited value if there is no way to monitor the usage.

2   Models for Identity Federation

Federated identity models are based on groups of *service providers* (SPs) that enter into a mutual security and authentication agreement in order to allow user SSO to their services. In the terminology of the Liberty Alliance, these groups are called *circles of trust* [3]. The user identity is asserted by one or more *identity providers* (IDPs). Identity federation can thus be defined as a set of agreements, standards and technologies that enable SPs to recognise user identities and entitlements from IDPs [7].

There are two particular approaches to organizing federations as well as scenarios where identity federation are combined. These will be discussed briefly in order to explore the need for user control in these scenarios.

2.1 The Hub-and-Spoke Model

The hub-and-spoke model for identity federation is where one or more centralized identity providers are federated with multiple separate service providers. This federation model is commonly found in environments with a degree of common management (e.g. governmental federations or umbrella companies). Note that service providers have no direct contact with each other within the federation context.

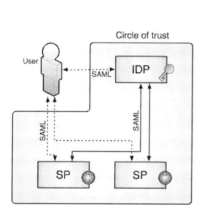 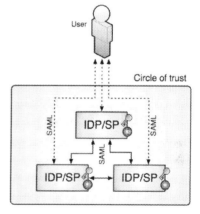

Fig. 1. Hub-and-spoke federation   **Fig. 2.** Dual-role SP-IDPs

With a typically low ratio of IDPs to SPs, the number and variation of assertions being transferred are quite limited. Users can potentially manage their federated identity by interacting with the central IDP(s), and therefore maintain an overview. Note that IDPs *can* also perform as SPs, although this is not often the case, due to mercantile reasons[1].

With x IDPs and y SPs, the user must manage up to $x \times y$ attribute combinations and account links. Whilst this may be challenging, it is at least feasible for such a federation to provide users with sufficient information. Note that the

---

[1] An IDP must often provide a high level of availability, support services, and test labs. The costs for this may be passed on to federated SPs in some way, which underlines the need to avoid mixing IDP and SP roles withing the same deployment.

SAML 2.0 specification does not include any standard protocol or requirement for the IDP to make federation information available to the user [1].

2.2   The SP-IDP Model

In the combined SP-IDP model, each SP also acts as an IDP, managing the name space of its own users whilst federating with the other SPs. Various silo identity domains are then linked together to form a federated domain [7], as shown in fig. 2. For authentication purposes, an SP will accept a *security assertion* [1] from another SP claiming that a given user has already been authenticated.

The ratio of IDPs to SPs in this model approaches 1:1. For each IDP in the circle of trust, there exists a set of attributes that can potentially be shared with other SPs. Furthermore, each IDP-SP relationship may be limited to a subset of the available attributes. This gives up to $x!$ attribute combinations and account links for the user to manage, where x is the number of dual-role SP-IDPs. Also, the lack of a single point of control[2] within the circle of trust prevents the user from effectively being able to manage or view these attribute combinations without visiting each and every IDP.

In such a model, it is difficult for the user to achieve a satisfactory overview of their federated identities. With increasing focus on privacy issues it is expected that privacy aspects of dual-role SP-IDP federations will have to be addressed in the near future.

2.3   Combining Identity Federations

Identity federations involve creating resonably tight trust and legal relationships. This limits the size of identity federations, and gives rise to the need for multiple federations. Whilst one may first address the need for informing and involving users *within* a federation, it is not particularly feasible for a user to have to check a multitude of Identity Dashboards in order to gain an overview of their federated identities. This gives rise to the notion of a cross-federation Identity Dashboard, capable of displaying information about many of the user's federations.

Multiple identity federations can also increase the need for the user to understand which attributes are being shared. For example, it is possible for a service provider to participate in two separate circles of trust (fig 3). If the user is presented with a choice of IDPs to authenticate to, information about which attributes would be shared may affect their decision.

Not only would the user have to relate to two different sources of information about their federated identity (IDP X and IDP Y), the user may also have trust issues based on which other SPs are involved in the respective circles of trust. For example, if a user does not trust the service provider SP 3 then they may not want to authenticate to IDP Y at all.

---

[2] There could well be more than one point of control (IDP) in a centralized model, so a single point of control is not necessarily a challenge restricted to dual-role SP-IDP federations.

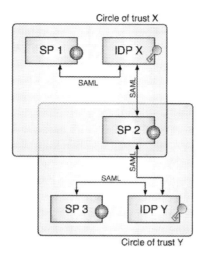

Fig. 3. Multiple circles of trust

3   Are Users Interested?

Before looking closer at what should be controlled, the question of whether a user is interested in how their identity attributes are handled should be addressed. A survey conducted by Ackerman et al. [10] asked American internet users how important it would be for them to be notified of privacy policy conflicts for different types of information or action (Table 1).

> If you could configure your web browser to look for privacy policies and privacy seals of approval on web sites and let you know when you were visiting a site whose privacy practices might not be acceptable to you, which criteria would be most important to you? For each of the items in the left-most column, please indicate whether it is very important, somewhat important, or not important. [10]

In this survey, a very significant proportion of users were interested in the sharing of information (79%), whether the information is identifiable (75%), and knowing the kind of information being handled (69%); all of these are relevant for a federated identity model.

In a separate survey by Earp et al [16], respondents were asked to state their agreement or disagreement with statements grouped into six categories of personal identity information events. These results were then ranked according to importance (Table 2). Also here, the transfer (sharing) of information and awareness of the information was considered more important that being able to alter or personalize it.

Both surveys find that the sharing of information is relatively important when compared with other uses and aspects of information privacy. The Identity

Table 1. Privacy Survey Results Ackerman et al. 1999

Information	Very important
Sharing of information	79%
Identifiable use of information	75%
Purpose of information collected	74%
Mailing list removal upon request	74%
Kind of information	69%
Access to stored information	65%
Site run by trusted company	62%
Posts privacy policy	49%
Privacy seal of approval	39%
Disclosure of data retention policy	32%

Table 2. Privacy Survey Results Earp et al. 2005

Category	Importance (rank)
Transfer	1
Notice/Awareness	2
Storage	3
Participation/Access	4
Collection	5
Personalization	6

Dashboard is accordingly focused on raising user awareness of the personal identity information being *shared*.

4   What a User Needs to Control

Identity federation involves sharing information across organizational borders. This information can include persistent identity attributes such as email addresses or social security numbers, and transient authentication information such as when and how you authenticated.

A typical federated authentication sequence based on SAML 2.0 is shown in figure 4 (redirects are not shown for the sake of simplicity). The following steps are involved[3]:

1. User attempts to access a service at SP site and is redirected to the appropriate IDP
2. IDP challenges the user to authenticate and redirects back to the SP
3. IDP issues a SAML assertion to the SP containing a unique identifier and user attributes
4. SP trusts assertion and uses the unique identifier to look up or create a local identity

---

[3] Assumes persistent federation in a service provider initiated single sign on scenario.

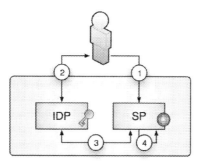

Fig. 4. Federated authentication

There are three key events in this sequence: the SP issues an authentication request to the IDP, a SAML assertion is issued, and a local account is looked up (or created). Additionally, the IDP-SP relationships established, and the names of these entities is relevant information.

An authentication request is a SAML message in which the SP details how the IDP should issue an assertion. A SAML assertion is a packet of security information including identity attributes and statements about how a user was authenticated. Looking up a local account requires that the user accounts on the IDP and the SP are, or have been, linked together. Users need to be able to find out which attributes are shared with which service providers, and should ideally be able to participate in making decisions about this.

4.1   Authentication Requests

When the user accesses a service provider site, which is a common way to initiate a federated authentication, the service provider sends an authentication request to the identity provider. The authentication request contains no personal information about the user, but does optionally provide some information about how the user identifier will be used. Of particular note is the name-id format which indicates whether a permanent link between a local account and the IDP user account will be used; known as *persistent* and *transient* identity federation. Other types of NameID exist, and are discussed is section 4.2. It is possible for both SP and IDP to support several NameID formats, one of which is chosen at runtime; the possible values can be found by interrogating the *MetaData* [1] configuration information for both parties.

There is also an ”AllowCreate” parameter that indicates whether the service provider wants to be able to create a local user profile based on the information passed later from the IDP. The intentions of the service provider can be relevant to users seeking to limit the number of personal accounts.

Thus, the two pieces of information judged relevant for end-users are whether transient or perisitent federation can be used, and whether the creation of local accounts on the service provider is allowed.

4.2 Assertions

Assertions, or more formally Security Asserions defined by the SAML v2 specifications, are where personal user data is exchanged. The assertion carries both the user identifier, *NameID* in SAMLv2 terminology, and user attributes. This information may be stored in a user profile on the IDP, dynamic information garnered from the authentication process, or third party information. Each assertion is addressed to an audience; a set of service providers.

Whilst the intended audience for an assertion can be of interest, it is very difficult to present this information in an understandable way to the user. There is no guarantee that the service provider will not pass on the information contained within the assertion, even if the actual assertion is only addressed to them. Audience is therefore judged not to be suitable for presentation to end-users.

The SessionIndex attribute to the AuthnStatement element can, in a privacy-wise poor implementation of the standard, contain user IDs, but this would be against the recommendation in the standard to use random impersonal values for the session index. Transfer of the session index is therefore not considered to be of interest to the user.

Likewise, the *NameID* value should be a random value for both persistent and transient formats, although other possible values are defined by the SAML v2 standards, including the use of email address, kerberos identifier, or x509 certificate distinguished name. These alternate, readable formats can be used if supported by both the IDP and the SP. This information is potentially of interest to the user, although rather than presenting the supported NameID formats, it is deemed easier to show the user the identifiers that are in use for each supported format. Note that transient identifiers are generated each time a session is created, so the values are indeterminate outside of a session.

Of prime importance to the user are the identity attributes; Attribute elements. Which attributes are exchanged can be reduced to a subset at runtime through the use of an *AttributeQuery*, but return by default all available attributes based on previous agreement. For example, in the OpenSSO SAML 2.0 implementation, the attributes available from the IDP and the attributes wanted by the SP are specified in extended metadata.

Thus, the information judged relevant to the end-users is the set of actual NameID identifiers that the IDP is prepared to use to identify the user to an SP, and critically the set of attributes that *may* be passed to the SP.

4.3 IDP-SP Relationships

Within a *circle of trust* relationships exist between each IDP and SP. These relationships are expressed through the use of MetaData. In terms of SAMLv2, MetaData is a concrete specification in the form of an xml schema. This specification exists so that there is a standard way to exchange federation configuration information.

Most of the information in MetaData describes how to interact with the entity (an IDP or SP). Locations define the URL target endpoints, bindings describe the protocols and channels for interacting with these endpoints, and the enclosing tags associate the individual transactions with a higher level *profile*.

These locations are not of direct interest to the user, although the bindings and protocols could be. There are a number of choices in the SAMLv2 standards which affect the level of security, such as whether authentication requests are signed, assertions encrypted, or whether endpoints are protected by transport-level security (SSL). However, evaluating the security strength of a federated system is not deemed realistically achievable for laymen. There is no known standard third-party evaluation of security strength that could be presented to users either.

MetaData contains a list of NameID formats that are accepted by each entity. Since it has already been proposed that actual NameID identifiers should be shown to users, the list of NameID formats need not be displayed and explained to the user.

Thus it is only the IDP-SP relationships themselves that are of interest to the user. To be able to present which IDPs will assert a user's identity to which SPs, we need to be able to name each entity. This is detailed in the next section.

4.4   IDP/SP Entity Identifiers

Each IDP or SP has an entity ID as defined by the SAMLv2 specification, and which has no verified human-readable name. An entity ID may not be recognisable to a user, or may be difficult to separate from other entities. For example: in a real federation a trend emerged whereby the IDP name was also the name of the federation project, and so many service providers used this as part of their SP entity ID. Ie (anonymized):

Table 3. Example entity IDs

IDP	bigidp.sample.org
SP 1	bigidp.another.org
SP 2	company-bigidp.company.com

Many of the existing products that support SAMLv2 federation will use the hostname of a server as the entity ID. This can lead to cryptic entity IDs such as "srv002-prod.brdg.company.com", which makes it harder for the user to understand which party is involved in the federation.

The accurate and secure translation of entity IDs is essential to providing users with the information and control they require. To address this issue, *nicknames* as defined by the *Petname System* [8] is proposed to give users a meaningful recognition of each entity involved.

The Petname System describes the process of naming people and entities in terms of security, memorability, and globalness. The system proposes the use of up to three names: a *key* which is global and secure, a *nickname* which is global and memorable, and a *petname* which is memorable and secure since each individual user sets their own petnames.

Since an entity ID accurately names an IDP or SP within a federation without being particularly memorable or understandable, this is a key. Rather than displaying to the user that "srv002-prod.brdg.company.com" is sending information to "idp.pqa.no" a more globally understandable name such as "The Norwegian Government" or "FlyMeFast Airlines IDP" should be used - this would be a nickname. Finally, a petname *could* be set in the dashboard by individual users to help them distinguish between entities with similar names; e.g. "My favourite airline". However, the main gain is perceived to be through the use of nicknames.

The SAML v2.0 specifications do not stipulate or facilitate the use of any identifier beyond the entity ID. Introducing a nickname in the Identity Dashboard would require gathering additional information about the identity and service providers and building up a local mapping of entity IDs to nicknames. However, nicknames would be equally useful within the federation for displaying information about which service provider the IDP is sending the user on to, for example. For this reason, the preferred solution is for each IDP to maintain a mapping to readable nicknames, and that these nicknames are communicated to the Identity Dashboard along with the information detailed above.

5   The Identity Dashboard

Having looked at identity federations and which information an end-user should ideally have access to, requirements can be stated for a proposed solution; a new component dubbed the *Identity Dashboard*. The Identity Dashboard is envisaged as a component that can be implemented alongside one or more network-based federations, and which would communicate with each IDP to collate information, and then present a web-based GUI to end-users where this information could be presented.

Figure 5 illustrates how the Identity Dashboard fits together with existing actors. Communication with end-users is via a web-based dashboard interface, whilst communication with IDPs would have to be standardized. In a SAML v2 context, then an extension or revision of the existing standards could be one approach. Alternately, a new standard with no dependencies on specific federation protocols could be created.

Based on the discussions above, there is a need for a solution which:

- Can collate information of interest for users
- Presents this information to users
- Provides a centralized information channel, both within and across federations, regardless of the federation model being used
- Can be trusted to give the user a better picture of their federated identity

The location of such a solution affects the requirements; a local dashboard application on the user's client machine would involve direct network contact between the client and each identity provider, client platform security would be a major factor, and mobility would have to be considered. A remotely hosted dashboard would require a 3rd party interested in providing such a service, and could potentially present a privacy threat if user identifiers are stored and/or used for other

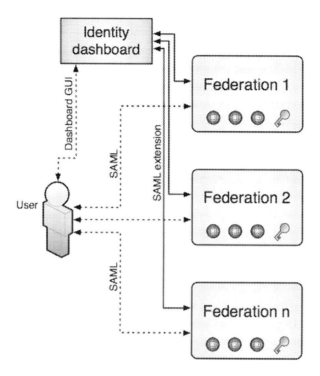

Fig. 5. Role of the Identity Dashboard

purposes by the dashboard. In this paper the Identity Dashboard is suggested as a common web-based component, although both approaches have their merits.

A proposed solution for handling these requirements is detailed in the following sections.

5.1   Collating Information

The following pieces of information were highlighted as relevant for users:

1. Name of participating entities (translation of entity IDs) per federation
2. List of the NameID identifiers that the IDP is prepared to use to identify the user in each IDP-SP relationship
3. List of attributes available in each IDP-SP relationship
4. Details of whether persistent or transient federation is supported and/or used for each IDP
5. Whether accounts will be created on-the-fly when a user performs a federated authentication without previously having an account
6. Additional *soft* information about each federation (rules, legal frameworks, contact details)

The IDPs in each federation are the datasource for all this information. Thus a connection between the Identity Dashboard, and the involved IDPs should be sufficient to garner this information. Note that due to privacy and security reasons, it is suggested that the Identity Dashboard should not store this information unless essential; information should be provided at runtime from each IDP at the request of the user.

As mentioned above, standardising how this information is retrieved from the IDPs is essential to realising the Identity Dashboard. The standard would also have to address security - how will the IDP know to release information to the dashboard? There are several approaches which could be considered, including using the ID-WSF and ID-SIS specifications from Liberty to create a new standard identity service which would retrieve this information. In such a scenario, the user would have to authenticate to an IDP in order to retrieve the relevant information. This would be a natural approach from a security perspective, although not particularly user-friendly as this would require the user to log in multiple times to access information.

The soft information (rules, legal frameworks, and contact details) is the only information that is not systematically available to the IDP. It is however natural that this information be made easily available and that the store for this information would be the IDP.

A prerequisite for the above to be true is that the Identity Dashboard must be aware of which identity federations the user participates in. A possible approach is for IDPs to register with the dashboard, where the dashboard acts as a discovery service. The user could then be presented with a list of known IDPs/federations, and asked to indicate those that are appropriate.

5.2   Presenting Information to Users

When the Identity Dashboard has securely collated information from one or more IDPs where the user has an account, the information must be presented to the user in an understandable way. The channel for presenting information is a web-based dashboard accessed over HTTPS. Figure 6 sketch showing the first step: selecting identity federations that the user participates in.

Beyond this, the user would potentially be required to authenticate to the IDP involved, whilst the Identity Dashboard negotiates with the IDP using ID-WSF. This step would be as per a normal login to the identity federation. Following this, the user would be presented with a list of relationships this IDP has with other SPs, and in a proxy federation, other IDPs. A proxy federation is where an IDP is itself a service provider, and which trusts a different IDP outside of the original circle of trust. See figure 7.

When a user wishes to look at an account link in more detail then clicking on a relationship should present the value and nature of the NameID identifiers, which user attributes are shared, and whether an account will be created for the user automatically on first-login. An example of this is shown in figure 8.

Fig. 6. Selecting federations where the user is active

Fig. 7. Relationships with the federation

A collated view showing selected details in a single table of federations and relationships would also be useful, although it would be expected to require multiple log-ins to the IDPs supplying information to the dashboard.

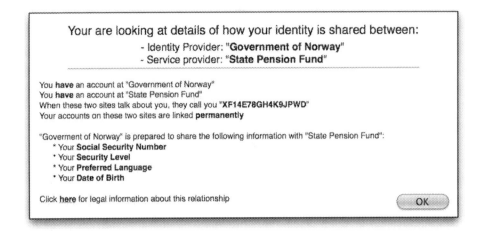

Fig. 8. Details of the IDP-SP relationship

6   Conclusion

The Identity Dashboard is presented as a possible approach to enabling users to control their federated identity. Should such a system be implemented, then there are a number of details and alternatives to consider that have not been fully explored in the scope of this paper. There are also some outstanding challenges.

As discussed in section 5, there are arguments for staging the Identity Dashboard on a web-based server or on the client system. Should extended standards be developed which would describe passing the necessary information from the IDPs to an Identity Dashboard, then both client-based and server-based dashboards would likely use the same protocols. The location is therefore not limited by the stance taken in this paper.

An aspect which is not further explored in this paper is to use the Identity Dashboard as a channel for interacting with end-users. Potential scenarios include acting as a Liberty ID-WSF interaction service, and providing standard tools for users to unlink accounts. A particularly relevant case is that user interaction during account linking is not covered by any Oasis or Liberty standard at this point in time. The implementation and design of such interaction can be difficult, and is often oversimplified reducing the number of decisions the use can make. In the worst case, account linkage may occur without the user being informed of the consequences at all. Could the Identity Dashboard play a watchdog role in account linking? These ideas are not currently included in the scope of the Identity Dashboard, but may be relevant for a server-based dashboard.

Central to the idea of the Identity Dashboard is passing information securely from an IDP to the dashboard. Asking the user to authenticate to the IDP as part of this process is presented as a possible solution, though user unfriendly. An alternative here could include viewing the Identity Dashboard as a valid identity provider in itself, which the target IDP trusts for the sole purpose of providing meta-information. This would however give rise to a number of security issues including account linking, trust issues, and increased security requirements of the Identity Dashboard itself. The question of authentication requires further exploration in order to find an optimal solution.

References

1. OASIS: Assertions and Protocols for the OASIS Security Assertion Markup Language (SAML) V2.0. OASIS (2005)
2. Microsoft/IBM: Web Services Federation Language Version 1.1. Microsoft/IBM (2006)
3. Liberty-Alliance: Liberty ID-FF Architecture Overview, version: 1.2-errata-v1.0. Liberty-Alliance (2003)
4. Shibboleth Project: Shibboleth Architecture Protocols and Profiles, Working Draft 05. Internet2/MACE (2004)
5. Squicciarini, A.C., Czeskis, A., Bhargav-Spantzel, A.: Privacy policies compliance across digital identity management systems. In: Proceedings of the SIGSPATIAL ACM GIS 2008 International Workshop on Security and Privacy in GIS and LBS, SPRINGL 2008, pp. 72–81. ACM, New York (2008)
6. Gevers, S., Verslype, V., De Decker, B.: Enhancing privacy in identity management systems. In: Proceedings of the 2007 ACM Workshop on Privacy in Electronic Society, WPES 2007, pp. 60–63. ACM, New York (2007)
7. Jøsang, A., AlZomai, M., Suriadi, S.: Usability and Privacy in Identity Management Architectures. In: The Proceedings of the Australasian Information Security Workshop (AISW). CRPIT, vol. 6. Australian Computer Society, Inc. (2007)
8. Stiegler, M.: http://www.skyhunter.com/marcs/petnames/IntroPetNames.html
9. Cranor, L.F., Guduru, P., Arjula, M.: User interfaces for privacy agents. ACM Trans. Comput.-Hum. Interact. 13(2), 135–178 (2006)
10. Ackerman, M.S., Cranor, L.F., Reagle, J.: Privacy in e-commerce: examining user scenarios and privacy preferences. In: Proceedings of the 1st ACM Conference on Electronic Commerce, EC 1999, pp. 1–8. ACM, New York (1999)
11. Ahn, G.-J., Lam, J.: Managing privacy preferences for federated identity management. In: Proceedings of the 2005 Workshop on Digital Identity Management, DIM 2005, pp. 28–36. ACM, New York (2005)
12. Microsoft, http://msdn.microsoft.com/winfx/reference/infocard/default.aspx
13. Higgins, http://www.eclipse.org/higgins
14. Ahn, G.-J., Ko, M., Shehab, M.: Privacy-enhanced User-Centric Identity Management. In: Proceedings of the IEEE International Conference on Communication. IEEE, Los Alamitos (2009)
15. Suriadi, S., Foo, E., Jøsang, A.: A User-centric Federated Single Sign-on System. In: 2007 IFIP International Conference on Network and Parallel Computing, IFIP (2007)
16. Earp, J.B., Antn, A.I., Aiman-Smith, L., Stufebeam, W.H.: Examining Internet Privacy Policies Within the Context of User Privacy Values. IEEE Transactions on Engineering Management (2005)

The Plateau:
Imitation Attack Resistance of
Gait Biometrics

Bendik B. Mjaaland

Accenture Technology Consulting - Security, Norway
bendik.mjaaland@accenture.com

Abstract. Constituting a new branch within biometrics, gait biometrics needs to be extensively tested and analyzed to determine its level of fraud resistance. Previous results examining the attack resistance testing of gait authentication systems show that imitation, or mimicking of gait, is a venerable challenge.

This paper presents an experiment where participants are extensively trained to become skilled gait mimickers. Results show that our physiological characteristics tend to work against us when we try to change something as fundamental as the way we walk. Simple gait details can be adopted, but if the imitator changes several characteristics at once, the walk is likely to become uneven and mechanical. The participants showed few indications of learning, and the results of most attackers even worsened over time, showing that training did nothing to help them succeed.

With extensive training an impostor's performance can change, but this change seems to meet a natural boundary, a limit. This paper introduces the **plateau**, a physiologically predetermined limit to performance, forcing imitators back whenever they attempt to improve further. The location of this plateau determines the outcome of an attack; for success it has to lie below the acceptance threshold corresponding to the Equal Error Rate (EER).

1   Introduction

Biometric technology has applications ranging from accessing ones computer to obtaining visa for international travel. The deployment of large-scale biometric systems in both commercial (e.g. Disney World [7], airports [2]) and government (e.g. US-VISIT [15]) applications has served to increase the public awareness of this technology. This rapid growth in biometric system deployment has clearly highlighted the challenges associated in designing and integrating these systems.

Biometric features are divided into two categories: physiological and behavioral biometrics. Physiological biometrics are characteristics that you cannot alter easily, they are stable parts or properties of your body. Examples are fingerprints, DNA, iris and retina. Behavioral characteristics can be altered and learned, such as gait, signature and keystroke dynamics. Within computer science, biometrics is often considered within the field of pattern recognition, and creating automated system approaches to such has been challenging [9].

E. de Leeuw, S. Fischer-Hübner, L. Fritsch (Eds.): IDMAN 2010, IFIP AICT 343, pp. 100–112, 2010.
© IFIP International Federation for Information Processing 2010

Recent advances in technology have shown us that we can automatically recognize individuals based on the way they walk. However, gait biometrics is a rather new area within biometrics, so the security of such technology needs to be challenged. Possibly the most intuitive threat towards gait biometrics is the mimicking attack, which is the topic of this paper. The reader should keep in mind that this is only one out of several attack points against biometric systems, a good reference here is [16], where Ratha et al. identified eight such attack points - imitation corresponding to number one in this research.

Contribution: Mjaaland et al. published research on gait mimicking in [11], and this paper extends this research. New insights to the imitator's challenges are presented, and conclusions are drawn on people's ability to adopt the gait characteristics of others. The term **plateau** is introduced, representing the natural boundary to an impostors performance in gait mimicking - as the title of this paper suggests.

This paper is organized as follows. Section 2 presents gait as a biometric feature and explains how it can be processed and analyzed. A description of Mjaaland's gait mimicking experiment is also included here. Section 3 introduces the plateau, and shows how to derive it using regression of impostor performance data. Section 4 presents the results, showing that single plateaus were discovered for almost all impostors. Finally, Section 5 and 6 presents conclusions and further work, respectively.

2   Gait Biometrics

2.1   Gait Analysis

The gait of a person is a periodic activity with each gait **cycle** covering two strides - the left foot forward and the right foot forward. It can also be split up into repetitive phases and tasks. Gait recognition has intrigued researchers for some time, already in the 1970's there were experiments done on the human perception of gait [9]. The first effort towards automated gait recognition (using machine vision) was probably done by Niyogi and Adelson [14] in the early 1990's. Several methods are known today, and we can categorize all known gait capturing methods into three categories [4]: machine vision based (MV), floor sensor based (FS) and wearable sensor based (WS).

Using wearable motion recording sensors to collect gait data is a rather newly explored field within gait biometrics. The earliest description of the idea known to the author is found in Morris' [12] PhD thesis from Harvard University in 2004. Since then, the academic community at Gjøvik University College (HiG) has devoted much effort researching gait biometrics. Gafurov's PhD work covers a broad part of WS-based gait recognition [4], and several students have written their master's thesis on the same topic [1,8,13,17].

WS-based gait collection has the advantage of being a rather unobtrusive way of collecting biometric data. It also has the immense advantage over MV of avoiding external noise factors such as camera placement and background or lighting issues. Furthermore, MV and FS is an expensive solution in terms of camera and floor equipment, while the WS do not require any infrastructure in the surroundings, and it is mobile.

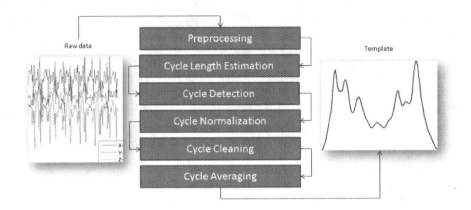

Fig. 1. Gait Analysis Overview

The best performance results have been achieved using WR technology, the best recorded to far is 2% [8], as opposed to 8% for MR and 65.8% for FS [5]. There are good reasons to choose WS, and this is the technology used in in the research presented in this paper. The analysis is based on the Cycle Length Method (CLM) developed by Gafurov [4] at Gjøvik University College. This method is essentially a framework on how to turn raw gait data into an averaged gait cycle of a fixed length. When the average cycle is found, this can be used as a user gait template.

The research presented in this paper is based on a self-developed software tool. The input to the tool is raw three-dimensional gait acceleration data, collected by wearable sensors attached to the hip. Data from the X, Y and Z direction constitute fragments of gait acceleration, which is combined into one resultant acceleration signal.

A high-level overview of the processing of raw gait data is shown in Figure 1. The first stage consists of preprocessing, where raw gait data is filtered and interpolated. The next three stages estimate the length of the cycles, detect their exact locations and normalizes them to the same length, respectively. The set of cycles is then cleaned (i.e. by removing outliers), and finally the average gait cycle is computed using simple averaging techniques.

The input to this algorithm typically consists of $10 - 20$ seconds of normal walk, and the final output is an average gait cycle, consisting of two strides - one for each foot. This average can be compared to other averages by well-known statistical distance metrics. Holien studied distance metric performance for gait biometrics in [8], and the superior metric, Dynamic Time Warping (DTW), is also used in the research presented here. The DTW method disposes the naturally occurring changes in walking speed and is able to compare signals of different lengths, and signals where the x-axis is shifted [8]. DTW can be used for various purposes, like for time-independent averaging, but in this research it was used simply as a distance metric. Algorithm details and MATLAB code used in this research can be found in [10].

2.2   The Mimicking Experiment

The research presented here is based on a mimicking experiment involving 50 participants, each enrolled with 10 templates, and 7 of these participated also as attackers.

The experiment is divided into three scenarios. The first is **the friendly scenario**, consisting of regular gait data from a test group of 50 participants. **The short-term and long-term hostile scenarios** are the two other scenarios, where a group of seven attackers attempted to imitate one specific victim. After each imitation attempt, the attacker was able to review his or her own gait on a video recording, and further improve the mimicking by comparing it to a video of the victim. A personal mimicking coach, or trainer, continuously assisted the attacker in the feedback process. Statistical results were also available. One session took about an hour, and five sessions were held for six "short-term" attackers, over a period of two weeks. The last attacker was the "long-term" attacker, having 20 sessions over six weeks.

The attackers and the victim in the two hostile scenarios were all selected from the friendly test group, and the attackers are referred to by numbering: A01, A03, A04, A18, A21, A38 and A41. The attackers were chosen such that their initial distances to the victim (i.e. the average distance between the victim's and the attacker's normal gait) consisted of both high and low values. Also, a reasonably stable gait was a requirement. In this regard the attackers represented "normal" people, with no specific advantages or disadvantages on average. Some anonymous non-sensitive details about the participants can be found in [10], but will not be included in this paper.

Two other mimicking experiments have been conducted, by Gafurov [6] and Stang [17]. However, these experiments are not extensive enough to provide valid indicators. Gafurov himself calls this part of his research a minimal-effort experiment, and in [10] Mjaaland presents a critique on both. In these experiments the participants do not conduct any structured training, and the search for *learning* is not properly conducted in either experiment.

The experiment described in this paper distinguishes itself from others by focusing on the attacker's mimicking skills, using sources of feedback like video capture and personal coaching to improve it. This investment of effort in impostor training has not been attempted in experiments before.

3   The Plateau: A Limit to Learning

As the experiment was conducted, attackers felt that despite that they sometimes improved performance, they found it very hard to improve beyond a certain point. This limit, or plateau, is described in this section. The actual results are presented in Section 4.

3.1 Plateau Characteristics

A plateau can be defined as "a state or period of little or no change following a period of activity or progress" [3], so on a learning curve it would correspond to the curve flattening out. Hence, observations concentrate around some value on the Y-axis, illustrated in the left part of Figure 2.

If exactly one plateau exists for each individual, then the success of an attacker is **predetermined** - the plateau has to lie below or near the acceptance threshold for an impostor to ever be able to succeed. How near it has to be depends on the variance in the data, as deviations potentially can be successful attacks.

The data in this experiment is not sufficient to make final conclusions on how the participants would be affected by an even more extensive training program. The uncertainty of the future is one of the reasons why the name "plateau" was chosen. If a temporary plateau is reached, and the performance later increases due to an extended training period, the term still makes sense. In this case one can imagine several plateaus belonging to the same performance plot, as illustrated in the right part of Figure 2. This situation should generate interesting questions, such as how to break through the different plateaus.

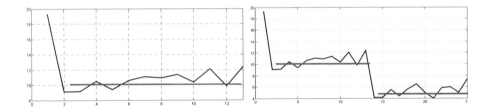

Fig. 2. Plateaus, conceptual illustration. A single plateau to the left, two to the right.

3.2 Analysis

Intuitively plateaus can be identified by looking at points of resistance, average values and converging curves. Coefficients from fitted "trend lines" can also be put to use for this purpose. Still, the most scientific way to find the plateau would be to look for a mathematical *limit*. The limit of a function tells us exactly where it is heading when x goes to infinity.

What separates the plateau from a mathematical limit should be addressed. While the limit is a purely mathematical concept that may or may not properly illustrate learning as we know it, the plateau opens for more human-like function behavior. The main difference is that a if a function exhibits a limit, only one such limit can exist. If only one plateau exists for an attacker, then the plateau and limit are identical. However, in the above it was suggested that an observed set of data points could exhibit several plateaus, and it would be valuable to study how each one could be "broken" if this was the case.

If several plateaus exist for an attacker, and the attacker is improving over time, then the lowest one will equal the limit. It is important to note that when statistical distance metrics are used, lower score means less separability, or difference, and higher mimicking performance. Hence, if the attacker is worsening his performance, the highest plateau equals the limit. In general we can refer to this as the final plateau.

The main objective of this research is to identify learning - in other words a systematic change in the performance of the attackers over time. A regression analysis was conducted for the purpose of finding a learning curve.

The regression model chosen for the analysis is based on an exponential curve:

$$Y(X) = \beta_1 + \beta_2 e^{\frac{\beta_3}{X}}, \tag{1}$$

where β_1, β_2 and β_3 are constants, the regression parameters, and $Y(X)$ is the estimate of observation X. This model removes natural fluctuations in performance, and also converges. The latter property is desirable because it corresponds to the fact that a learning process normally has a limit to its effect. It will also simplify the process of identifying plateaus.

Final (and single) plateaus are identified by taking the mathematical limit of the learning curve:

$$\rho_{nm} = \lim_{x \to \infty} Y_{nm}(X), \tag{2}$$

where where ρ_{nm} is the plateau of participant nm (e.g. 01 for A01), and Y is the learning curve of that participant.

4   Results

4.1   Performance

The Decision Error Tradeoff (DET) curve shows system performance in terms of different thresholds, and the relationship between False Match Rate (FMR) and False Non-Match Rate (FNMR) in the system [8]. The curve is constructed by performing pairwise comparisons between all 500 templates enrolled in the system. The left part of Figure 3 shows the DET curve for the mimicking experiment. The Equal Error Rate (EER) is 6.2%, corresponding to an acceptance threshold of $T = 8.6449$. Since performance optimization was not the objective of this reserch, these results were indeed good enough to proceed. Also, by not lowering the EER further the attackers had an easier task, which is a scientific advantage in this case.

The right part of Figure 3 shows an example of mimicking results. As these results are measured using a statistical distance metric, downward sloping regression curves indicate improving results. For example, two identical gait samples

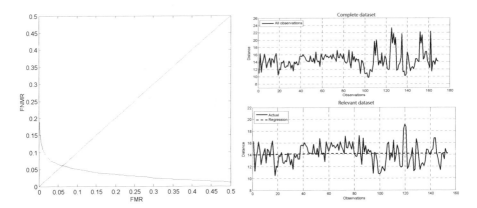

Fig. 3. Left: DET curve, friendly scenario, EER = 6.2%. Right: Long-term attacker A01 regression analysis.

yield a mimicking score of zero. The threshold of acceptance in this research is at $T = 8.6449$, so for the attacker to succeed he or she would have to exhibit a learning curve converging to a point below this value.

The example in Figure 3 is from the regression analysis of the long-term attacker A01. The dotted regression line is given by $Y_{01}(X) = 13.9962 + 0.2588e^{\frac{-19.8894}{X}}$, representing the learning curve. In this case the curve is rising, indicating worsening performance. Using confidence intervals for the parameters β_1 and β_2, we can calculate a window of 95% certainty where the attacker is heading over time. The regression line of A01 converges to $\rho_{01} = 14.2550$, significantly higher than the acceptance threshold. The 95% confidence interval of this particular attacker is $[11.7599; 16.7501]$, so not even the most optimistic forecast yields a sufficiently low result for this attacker. More numeric results are found in [11].

Four out of seven attackers **worsened** their performance during training (A01, A04, A21 and A38), in other words - they were better off when they did not try at all. None of these were near the acceptance threshold, even according to the most optimistic forecasts. The analysis also shows that only two attackers (A03, A18) improved their performance, exhibiting downward sloping curves. The final attacker, A41, has an ill-defined regression curve with no obvious interpretation. However, all of these results are relevant and will be discussed in this paper.

4.2   Single Plateaus

As mentioned above two attackers improved during their training, A18 and A03, and their results are plotted in Figure 4 and 5, respectively. A03's performance was fluctuating around his plateau from the very beginning. Looking at his performance plot it can be seen that it is mostly his variance that changes. Very large fluctuations can be seen in the beginning, while at point A the results stabilize. A03 learned to focus on the particular characteristics of his gait that gave the best results, concentrating his result values around the plateau.

During the last 10 - 15 attempts, starting at point B in the figure, he decided to introduce more changes. This resulted in more fluctuations in both directions, but never produced stable improvement. A03 reported difficulty combining gait characteristics, and felt that he ended up walking in an unnatural way.

A18 will be used for numeric examples; his regression curve is defined as $Y_{18}(X) = 10.2662 - 2.0549e^{\frac{-22.3333}{X}}$. By also looking at the result plot, the reader can easily verify that this attacker is improving. His learning curve converges to $\rho_{18} = 8.2113$, which makes him the only successful impostor in the experiment. A03's curve converges to a limit above the acceptance threshold, $\rho_{03} = 10.5176$. For the complete regression analysis of A18, see Table 1.

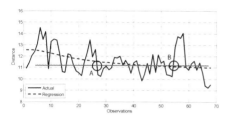

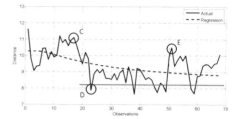

Fig. 4. Attacker A03 learning curve superimposed on the data set. The straight line is the plateau, the attacker managed to stabilize his results here between point A and B.

Fig. 5. Attacker A18 learning curve superimposed on the data set. The straight line is the plateau, first reached at point D.

Although A18 did improve his performance, this improvement is mainly occurring between point C and D in Figure 5. After point D, the decreasing values seem to meet resistance, a performance boundary. The mathematical limit of the regression curve confirms diminishing improvement. A single plateau is found at the limit, 8.2113, with a 95% confidence interval of $[6.6288 < \rho_{18} < 9.7939]$.

When A18 realized that he had problems improving further, he made some radical changes to his gait. This made his walk mechanical and uneven, and eliminated some previously adopted gait characteristics. In the plot this can be seen, starting at point E with a significant increase, followed by high fluctuations and instability for the rest of the training. Such observations were made also for other attackers - significant changes of the gait seemed to neutralize previous improvement and acquired skill.

A18 was the success story, as he learned enough to break the threshold. However, this was not the case for the other participants. The four participants that worsened their performance, A01, A04, A21 and A38, had their plateaus identified at $14.2550, 14.8051, 13.1676$ and 13.3554, respectively. These results are significantly higher than the acceptance threshold. Figure 6 provides an illustration for A01 and A21.

Table 1. Regression analysis for attacker A18. The regression curve converges to a plateau at 8.2113, and the curve is verified using the regression of the residuals and a hypothesis test [10].

Regression model	$Y(X) = \beta_1 + \beta_2 e^{\frac{\beta_3}{X}}$
Regression curve	$Y_{18}(X) = 10.2662 - 2.0549 e^{\frac{-22.3333}{X}}$
Limit / Plateau	8.2113
β_1 95% confidence interval	$9.6371 < \beta_1 < 10.8953$
β_2 95% confidence interval	$-3.0083 < \beta_2 < -1.1015$
Plateau 95% confidence interval	$6.6288 < \rho_{18} < 9.7939$
MSE	0.6503
Residual regression model	$Y(X) = \lambda_1 + \lambda_2 X$
Residual regression curve	$Y_{18}(X) = -0.1179 + 0.0034X$
λ_2 confidence interval 95%	$-0.0064 < \lambda_2 < 0.0133$
Residual MSE	0.6358
H_0	$\lambda_2 = 0$
H_0 P-value	0.4901 (Failed to reject H_0)

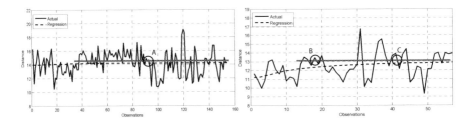

Fig. 6. The discovered plateaus of A01 (left) and A21 (right)

The effects of the plateaus were striking. Attacker A01 found an unnatural walk that sometimes gave better results compared to what his plateau suggested. It turned out, even if that particular walk was a better way of mimicking, he could not stabilize it. On the figure this can be seen starting at point A. The variance increased and the attacker lost control of the previously improved gait characteristics, and the plateau kept forcing A01's performance back.

A21 was the attacker with the least control of his gait. Most of the time he experienced problems when trying to change characteristics of his walking, and the reader may verify this looking at the high variation in his results. His worsening performance did sometimes stabilize around the plateau, around point B and C.

There were significant differences between the participants in terms of *how* they reached their plateau. The three attackers A03, A18 and A38 changed the most during the training, producing steeply sloped learning curves. Obviously this does not necessarily mean they increased their skills, just that their original score was far away from the plateau. Other attackers, like the long-term attacker A01, intitially got results very close to their plateaus, and thus found it a lot harder to improve beyond that point.

Furthermore, one can ask whether or not a higher plateau, where a performance *decrease* hits a boundary, is less interesting than a plateau reached after an *increase* of performance. No matter what direction the learning curve takes, it reflects the ability of the attacker to change his walk into something different, and keep it stable. When it comes to learning we are interested mainly in how far away the plateau is from the initial few mimicking attempts.

The results show that it is possible to slightly improve the performance of gait mimicking using training and feedback. By experimenting with small and large changes of gait characteristics, two attackers did move somewhat closer to the victim. However, the performance increase shown is very limited. It was clear that the attackers met their natural boundaries and had huge problems moving on from that point. This indicates that even if you can train to adopt certain characteristics of your victim, the outcome of your attempt is predetermined by your plateau. If it lies too high, you will never be able to mimic that person. And most attackers actually experienced worsening performance, converging towards a plateau far above the acceptance threshold.

4.3 Breaking Through

It is useful to look at the possible existence of several plateaus simultaneously, challenging the assumption of a predetermined attack outcome. Looking at the plot for A41 in Figure 7, two plateaus are superimposed, illustrating a plateau break in point A. Notice the sharp decline of the regression curve after the break; this curve is converging to a negative value. We cannot calculate the second plateau directly due to this ill-defined regression result, hence the lines are not mathematically derived and are provided for illustration only.

We may also want to re-interpret A18's performance plot in Figure 5, and add a second plateaus as shown in Figure 8. This attacker was initially producing very static results, indicating a plateau, but at point C the results began to improve. This improvement reached more resistance around point D. Reaching the new plateau represented a significant improvement, although A18's performance also became unstable. In fact it may seem like A18 returned to his original plateau in point E.

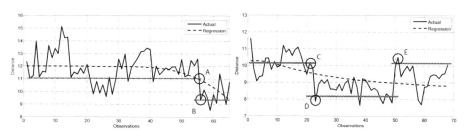

Fig. 7. A41's results, showing a possible plateau break at point A, and a new plateau reached at point B.

Fig. 8. A re-interpretation of A18's results, with a possible plateau break at point C, a new plateau at point D, and a return to the original plateau in point E.

The reader should note that the multi-plateau observations here are uncertain. Not enough data is available to support any claims on several plateaus, and the results have very high fluctuations in the areas of possible plateau breaks. A more plausible explanation would be that the "real" plateau is the second, or final plateau, and that the first is caused by noise from poor mimicking. Furthermore, the research also indicated that the assumed new plateau was very hard to reach, and that the degree of learning was inadequate to pose a real threat. Even with many plateaus, reaching the second requires extreme effort, and any proceeding plateaus are likely to be harder to reach than the one before.

5   Conclusions

This paper looked at fraud resistance of gait biometrics with respect to imitation, or mimicking attacks. The research showed that learning to walk like someone else is very difficult, and that there is a limit to the attacker's performance that causes the attack results to be predetermined. Either the attacker's normal walk, with a slight training adjustment, is close enough to that of the victim, or it is not. Extensive training, even with coaching and continuous feedback, does not seem to change this outcome.

The attackers hit a natural boundary that prevented them from improving their performance beyond a certain point. The effect of this phenomenon was striking, and given a name: a plateau.

We presented research on gait mimicking in [11], where an experiment was conducted with a specific objective in mind - increasing attackers imitation skills. This was attempted using various forms of training and feedback, tailored to see if the ability to mimic gait can change over time.

The main part of the experiment was "hostile", with attackers training to imitate the gait of the same victim. The participants did not show significant improvement or learning overall. A regression analysis was conducted in order to establish this fact - most learning curves were sloping upwards, indicating worsening performance.

With the research of this paper it was found that training has little or no effect on the plateau, it seems to be a physiologically predetermined boundary to every individual's mimicking performance. If only one such plateau exists, then it is mathematically the same as a limit, in essence - the value to which the learning curve converges. Natural fluctuations will be present, but the average results will approach the plateau over time.

A single plateau was identified for all attackers with an interpretable regression curve. However, it was speculated on whether or not individuals can exhibit more than one plateau. This is partly why the term plateau was chosen in the first place - it is not as strict as the mathematical definition of a limit.

To succeed in a mimicking attack with a single plateau, the plateau itself must lie below or close to the threshold of acceptance. That is, natural fluctuations may cause some successful attempts even if the plateau is above the threshold. This depends on the variance of the gait. Only one attacker (A18) posed a direct threat to the victim.

In order to succeed in a mimicking attack with several plateaus, the attacker has to reach a plateau that has the same properties as the one described above - close to or below the threshold. Little data suggested that multiple plateaus can exist simultaneously, but even if it could it is also likely that plateaus get harder to break the closer to the threshold they are.

It should be noted that the findings of this paper cannot necessarily be generalized to apply to other analysis methods. The results here applies to the combination of methods and configurations presented. However, a lot of the difficulties in gait mimicking are likely to be physiologically rooted, and thus it is reasonable to assume that the indicators are relevant in other contexts as well.

Summarized, the attackers had varying skills and results, and only one of them got to a plateau below the threshold. If we consider a future improvement in gait biometrics, that one attacker is a neglible threat. What is much more important - the attackers hardly learned at all. Their improvements were mostly insignificant, and they struggled hard to be free of their plateaus.

6   Further Work

There are various possibilities for future work on gait biometrics. For gait mimicking in particular - this research cannot provide final answers because the data set is not large enough, and not all the results can be generalized. More experiments are needed, with different methods, more test subjects and more extensive training. In particular, extended time frames and more training would be the key to get a definite conclusion on the single/multiple plateau issue.

Different results might be achieved if the gait analysis scheme is significantly changed. For instance, if Fast Fourier Transformation (FFT) was used in order to look on gait in the frequency domain, we might see other trends and characteristics in the attackers performance. A large part of the observations are generalizable - for instance that physiological boundaries makes gait mimicking difficult, but we cannot claim that our observations hold under all circumstances. A future task could be to perform the same experiment with different analysis tools.

It would be interesting to get precise physiological explanations on *why* it is so hard to imitate other peoples walks. For this, anatomical and medical studies would have to come into play, and a successful report on the topic would definitely strengthen the documented security of gait biometrics.

Other aspects of mimicking could also be analyzed - like threats through cooperation. Cooperation in gait mimicking essentially means that two people try to walk like each other, and then maybe "meet in the middle". Hence, one person could enroll walking somewhat like a different person and, if successful, they could both authenticate with the same template.

It would be beneficial to try to identify so-called sheep and wolf characteristics within gait biometrics. Some people may be easier targets for imitation, "sheep", and some people may be better at impersonating than others, "wolves". Further, such (dis)advantages could be genetically determined, and these issues together can form entire new lines of research within gait mimicking.

On the field of gait biometrics in general there is a lot of work to do. The performance of gait recognition systems are not generally competitive to other biometrics at the time of writing, so the invention of new methods, and further development of the existing methods is necessary.

References

1. Buvarp, T.E.: Hip movement based authentication - how will imitation affect the results? Master's thesis, Gjøvik University College - Department of Computer Science and Media Technology (2006)
2. Clarke, R.: Biometrics in airports how to, and how not to, stop mahommed atta and friends (2003),
   http://www.anu.edu.au/people/Roger.Clarke/DV/BioAirports.html
3. Oxford Dictionaries. Compact Oxford English Dictionary of Current English, 3rd edn. (2005)
4. Gafurov, D.: Performance and Security Analysis of Gait-based User Authentication. PhD thesis, University of Oslo (2008)
5. Gafurov, D., Snekkenes, E., Bours, P.: Gait authentication and identification using wearable accelerometer sensor. In: Proceedings of the IEEE Workshop on Automatic Identification Advanced Technologies, AutoID (2007)
6. Gafurov, D., Snekkenes, E., Bours, P.: Spoof attacks on gait authentication system. Special Issue on Human Detection and Recognition (2007)
7. Harmel, K., Spadanuta, L.: Disney world scans fingerprint details of park visitors. The Boston Globe (September 3, 2006)
8. Holien, K.: Gait recognition under non-standard circumstances. Master's thesis, Gjøvik University College - Department of Computer Science and Media Technology (2008)
9. Jain, A.K., Flynn, P., Ross, A.A.: Handbook of Biometrics, vol. 556. Springer, US (2008)
10. Mjaaland, B.B.: Gait mimicking - attack resistance testing of gait authentication systems. Master's thesis, Norwegian University of Science and Technology, NTNU (2009)
11. Mjaaland, B.B., Bours, P., Gligoroski, D.: Gait mimicking - attack resistance testing of gait authentication systems. In: Proceedings of the 2nd Norwegian Information Security Conference, NISK 2009, NISNet, Tapir Akademiske Forlag, Trondheim, Norway (2009)
12. Morris, S.J.: A shoe-integrated sensor system for wireless gait analysis and real-time therapeutic feedback. PhD Thesis, Harvard University - MIT Division of Health Sciences and Technology (2004)
13. Søndrol, T.: Using the human gait for authentication. Master's thesis, Gjøvik University College - Department of Computer Science and Media Technology (2005)
14. Nixon, S.A., Adelson, E.H.: Analylzing gait with spatiotemporal surfaces. In: Proceedings of IEEE Workshop on Non-Rigid Motion (1994)
15. U.S. Department of State. Safety and security of u.s. borders/biometrics. State official online information (2008)
16. Ratha, N.K., Connell, J.H., Bolle, R.M.: An analysis of minutiae matching strength. IBM Thomas J. Watson Research Center (2001)
17. Stang, Ø.: Gait analysis: Is it easy to learn to walk like someone else? Master's thesis, Gjøvik University College - Department of Computer Science and Media Technology (2007)

Privacy-Friendly Incentives and Their Application to Wikipedia*

Jan Camenisch[1], Thomas Groß[1], Peter Hladky[2,**], and Christian Hoertnagl[1]

[1] IBM Research - Zurich, Rüschlikon, Switzerland
[2] Department of Computer Science, ETH Zurich, Switzerland

Abstract. Double-blind peer review is a powerful method to achieve high quality and thus trustworthiness of user-contributed content. Facilitating such reviews requires incentives as well as privacy protection for the reviewers. In this paper, we present the concept of privacy-friendly incentives and discuss the required properties. We then propose a concrete cryptographic realization based on ideas from anonymous e-cash and credential systems. Finally, we report on our software's integration into the MediaWiki software.

Keywords: anonymous credentials, pseudonyms, e-cash, privacy, anonymity.

1   Introduction

We, as users, all rely increasingly on information on the Internet, ranging from stock quotes and financial news to medical information. Also, businesses and organizations (including governments) rely on information on the Internet to make their decisions—including, for instance, court cases and financial investments. It is therefore crucial that this information can be trusted to be correct.

Information provided by organizations is typically considered trustworthy because organizations are trusted to have quality assurance processes in place. Moreover, they can be held liable for publishing incorrect information. An increasing part of the Internet's content is *user-contributed*. Here, assessing the trustworthiness of the information is much more difficult, because the contributing users are typically barely known and can easily be impersonated. Also, as they can hardly be held liable, users sometimes contribute wrong information, on purpose. Such cases range from discrediting other users to manipulating votes or markets, see [25,26] for examples.

Sites such as Wikipedia try to address this problem by establishing user's reputation. This is normally done by registration and *identification of the users*, sacrificing users' privacy for the quality of their contributions. For instance, Citizendium, a new electronic encyclopedia project, only accepts contributors who are registered with full curriculum vitae and proof of identity. The contributors must consent to obligatory disclosure of their Personal Identifiable Information (PII). However, users often prefer to be anonymous or pseudonymous when contributing contents or commenting on other

---

* The extended version of this paper is available in the Cryptology ePrint Archive [6].
** Work done during internship at IBM Research - Zurich.

E. de Leeuw, S. Fischer-Hübner, L. Fritsch (Eds.): IDMAN 2010, IFIP AICT 343, pp. 113–129, 2010.

contributions. In fact, it is crucial for protecting all our on-line privacy to be able to interact with such wide on-line communities in an anonymous or pseudonymous way. Moreover, pseudonymous interactions generally seem to guarantee higher quality of contributions.

An additional mechanism for quality assurance is *distributed moderation or rating* as, for instance, used by Slashdot.org or Apple's App store for the iPhone. Distributed moderation is typically done by rating, tagging, and reviewing of contributions or, in other words, by adding meta-data of the user community itself. It seems that such systems can quickly and consistently separate high and low quality comments in an online conversation [18], but also that the quantity and quality of meta-data may not be sufficient in practice unless users are given sufficient incentives. The latter was also observed in an experiment made on the IBM Intranet as part of the PrimeLife project [22]. Incentives could be in the form of monetary payments (e.g., micro-payments or points that can be redeemed later for a book or CD), valuations such as gaining reputation (cf. eBay), or in the form of side-effects (e.g., as games with a purpose [2]).

In conclusion, we need an on-line collaboration system that, on the one hand, protects the privacy of the users and, on the other hand, enhances the quality by giving incentives for reviews and moderation. For the latter, we need of course to ensure that the privacy offered cannot be abused. For instance, it must not be possible that one and the same person provides the original contribution and then also does all the moderation and reviews. In the paper, we first investigate the requirements and then provide a system that offers maximal privacy to the users, and allows for providing incentives and the establishment of reputations. Our system is based on unlinkable pseudonyms, anonymous credentials and e-cash [19,4,7,8].

Contributions. We specify the first privacy-friendly incentive system with strong privacy protection and accountability. The system not only covers incentives and reputation, but also separation of duties, role-based and attribute-based entitlement policies. We provide a cryptographic realization based on abstract interfaces with zero-knowledge proofs of knowledge, anonymous credential systems and anonymous e-cash as primitives. Our system can be instantiated in the Strong RSA (SRSA) as well as in the Elliptic Curve Cryptography (ECC) setting.

We have implemented our incentive system for Wikipedia using the Identity Mixer cryptographic library [17] based on the SRSA. It can be used with any other on-line collaboration platform. We intend to make our source code publicly available at [22].

2   Privacy-Friendly Incentives

Wikipedia provides documents to its users contributed by members of the community. This user-generated content varies in quality and can be significantly improved by (expert) reviews and comments. As most scientists know, good reviews are time-consuming, that is, come at a cost. Even though community service out of idealism is a common trait in the Wikipedia community, incentive systems can improve the situation for contributors as well as for the contributed content. They aim at reimbursing the review or revision cost by awards, and at invigorating the review process.

Privacy-friendly incentives complement this fundamental goal with anonymity and privacy protection for all users. Therefore, they enable a double-blind peer review process and nurture fairness, impartiality, and rigor. Authors as well as the reviewers of documents can remain anonymous during the entire review process. Such a review process is believed to be essential for academic quality, even though it sometimes lacks in reviewer accountability. Our goal is to establish a cryptographic system that reaches high quality standards, while fulfilling the diverse requirements of the involved parties.

We formalize the incentive system as a collaborative document editing system, in which all revisions, reviews and comments are linked to one initial document P_0. We consider a document version history $\mathbb{P} = \{P_0, \ldots P_n\}$ as ordered sequence of revisions, reviews and comments associated with the P_0, where P_n denotes the most recent revision or review.

Principals. There are multiple parties interacting with a document P. We have a clearing house that hosts all documents and organizes the incentive system, in our case the wiki W component. The wiki has a community of users and each user U may act in different and multiple roles:

Reader U: A reader consumes a document P. Any reader may offer incentives to other users to improve the quality of a document by a review or a revision.

Author V: An author contributes an initial version or a revision of a document P.

Reviewer R: A reviewer contributes reviews and comments for a document P in exchange for receiving an incentive.

Editor E: An editor is a privileged user, who may approve or decline document revisions or reviews by authors and reviewers.

We introduce a bank B to exchange electronic incentives for real-world goods and awards. Users of wiki W can withdraw fresh incentive e-coins and deposit spent ones as part of our virtual incentive economy. Even though we allow a system with full anonymity, we require each user to register with a trusted identity issuer I to infuse accountability in the entire review and incentive process. Each user U obtains an identity certificate σ_U on its identity sk_U from issuer I. Our system works with multiple banks as well as multiple identity issuers, we focus on the single-bank/single-issuer case for simplicity. The identity of an honest user is never revealed by the incentive system, whereas the certified identity enforces separation of duties between authors and reviewers, and prevents double-spending attacks as well as vandalism.

Concepts. In a privacy-friendly incentive system, many anonymous users interact with a single document P. Incentives may be given before or after a contribution (revision or review). *Pre-contribution* incentives are offered to users to provide a contribution at all and it is independent from the contribution quality. For instance, a reader U can offer incentive e-coins for any reviewer R who is willing to contribute a review. *Post-contribution* incentives are offered after the contribution is made and may be dependent on the quality of the contribution. For instance, users can rate the quality of reviewer's contribution and offer reputation e-coins for his work.

In our model, a reader U explicitly withdraws incentives from a bank B. The reader U offers these *pre-contribution* incentives on the wiki W for improvements on a document P. The wiki W acts as a clearing house and it is responsible for ensuring unlinkability by exchanging the spent incentives of reader U with bank B for fresh incentives. Once a reviewer R decides to contribute a review P', he submits the review to the wiki W for inspection by an editor E. Once the editor E approves the review, the reviewer R can obtain the incentives from the wiki W. We leave community approval to the extensions in Sect. 5. As *post-contribution* incentives extension, the number of obtained incentives can be dependent on the review rating or the reviewer can obtain separate reputation e-coins to build a reputation credential.

Checks and Balances. The privacy-friendly incentive system provides anonymity to all users and balances this property with strong accountability safe-guards. In a fully anonymous system without such safe-guards, malicious users could attempt to manipulate reviews, sabotage other author's work or publish fabrications without accountability. Well known examples of checks and balances to counter those attacks are the separation of reviewer and author/editor, or the binding of reviews and documents to the contributor's true identity.

To achieve accountability as well as separation of duties between roles, we introduce a cryptographic domain pseudonym $N_{P,U}$ for each user U that interacts with a document P. It is a function of the user's true identity sk_U and the document P while hiding sk_U computationally. Therefore, each entity interacting with document P has one unique pseudonym, which is independent from entity's role. Pseudonyms $N_{P,U}$ and $N_{Q,U}$ created for different documents P and Q are unlinkable.

3   Preliminaries

In this section we describe the abstract interfaces of the cryptographic primitives we employ, mostly following Bangerter et al. [4]. Our actual implementation uses and extends the Identity Mixer library [17] which offers the following primitives.

3.1   Commitment Schemes

A commitment scheme allows one to commit to a message m from some domain (typically $\mathbb{Z}_q$ for some prime q). The interface is as follows.

$C \leftarrow \mathsf{Commit}(m, r)$: Commit to message m via commitment C.
$\{0, 1\} \leftarrow \mathsf{VerifyCommit}(C, m, r)$: Verify commitment C belonging to message m.

The interface can be instantiated by the Pedersen commitment scheme [21] or the Integer commitment scheme by Damgård and Fujisaki [12]. For the Pedersen scheme, public parameters are a group G of prime order q, and generators $(g_0, \ldots, g_l)$. In order to commit to the values $(m_1, \ldots, m_l) \in \mathbb{Z}_q^l$, pick a random $r \in \mathbb{Z}_q$ and set

$$C \leftarrow \mathsf{Commit}((m_1, \ldots, m_l), r) = g_0^r \prod_{i=1}^{l} g_i^{m_i} \ .$$

3.2 Zero-Knowledge Proofs and Σ-Protocols

When referring to the zero-knowledge proofs of knowledge of discrete logarithms and statements about them, we will follow the notation introduced by Camenisch and Stadler [11] and formally defined by Camenisch, Kiayias, and Yung [9].

For instance, $PK\{(a, b, c) : y = g^a h^b \wedge \tilde{y} = \tilde{g}^a \tilde{h}^c\}$ denotes a *"zero-knowledge Proof of Knowledge of integers a, b and c such that $y = g^a h^b$ and $\tilde{y} = \tilde{g}^a \tilde{h}^c$ holds,"* where $y, g, h, \tilde{y}, \tilde{g}$ and $\tilde{h}$ are elements of some groups $G = \langle g \rangle = \langle h \rangle$ and $\tilde{G} = \langle \tilde{g} \rangle = \langle \tilde{h} \rangle$. Following the approach of Bangerter et al., the PK notation accepts abstract predicates on input. For instance, $PK\{(m, r) : \text{VerifyCommit}(C, m, r)\}$ denotes the proof of representation of a commitment. SPK denotes a signature proof of knowledge, that is a non-interactive transformation of a proof with the Fiat-Shamir Heuristic [14].

3.3 Signature Scheme for Anonymous Credentials

Bangerter et al. [4] formalize anonymous credential systems as an abstract signature interface. The signer is an issuer I with a key pair (sk_I, pk_I).

$(sk_I, pk_I) \leftarrow \text{SetupSig}(\ell)$: Key generation for the issuer I.

$(\sigma)() \leftarrow \text{HiddenSign}((C_1, \dots, C_{l'}), (m_{l'+1}, \dots m_l), r; pk_I)(sk_I)$: Issuer I signs hidden messages $(m_1, \dots, m_{l'})$ in commitments $(C_1, \dots, C_{l'})$ as well as known messages $(m_{l'+1}, \dots, m_l)$. The user completes the signature σ with the commitment randomness r.

$\{0, 1\} \leftarrow \text{VerifySig}(\sigma, (m_1, \dots, m_l); pk_I)$: Predicate to verify a signature σ by issuer I on messages $(m_1, \dots, m_l)$.

$\{0, 1\} \leftarrow \text{VerifySigPred}(\sigma, (m_1, \dots, m_l), \text{AttrPredicate}; pk_I)$: Verifies additionally that the efficiently provable predicate AttrPredicate over the messages $(m_1, \dots, m_l)$ is fulfilled.

This abstraction contains the following key points: First, it provides a HiddenSign() function that allows an issuer I to sign committed values $C_i = \text{Commit}(m_i, r)$, $i \in \{1, \dots, l'\}$ without knowledge of the hidden values m_i. Second, it provides a predicate VerifySig() that allows for a verification of signatures in zero-knowledge proofs of knowledge. Third, it offers an additional predicate VerifySigPred() to verify attribute statements over the attributes of signature σ in zero-knowledge proofs.

3.4 E-Coin Schemes

Our construction uses simple e-coins as a basic building block. We reference compact e-cash [8] for a formal set of definitions.

$(sk_B, pk_B) \leftarrow \text{SetupBank}(\ell)$: Key generation for a bank B.

$(\sigma_\Psi, d_\Psi, s_\Psi)() \leftarrow \text{Withdraw}(\sigma_U; sk_U, pk_B)(sk_B, pk_I)$: User U withdraws an unspent e-coin $(\sigma_\Psi, d_\Psi, s_\Psi)$ from a bank B, where σ_Ψ is the bank's signature on the e-coin, d_Ψ is a double-spending random element and s_Ψ is the e-coin serial number. The bank verifies U's identity sk_U certified by issuer I in signature σ_U.

$(T, R)(\Psi) \leftarrow \mathsf{Spend}(\sigma_U, (\sigma_\Psi, d_\Psi, s_\Psi); sk_U)(pk_B)$: User U spends an e-coin $(\sigma_\Psi, d_\Psi, s_\Psi)$ with a recipient while proving ownership of the e-coin with relation to its identity sk_U. The recipient outputs a spent e-coin $\Psi = (s_\Psi, R, T, \Phi)$, where R is a challenge from the recipient, T is a function of (sk_U, R, d_Ψ) such that $T \leftarrow g_B^{sk_U R} g_B^{d_\Psi}$ is computed by the user U and Φ is the proof transcript.

$()(\Psi) \leftarrow \mathsf{Deposit}(\Psi)()$: Sends a spent e-coin Ψ to the bank B.

$(pk_U, \Pi) \leftarrow \mathsf{Identify}(\Psi_1, \Psi_2)$: Bank B runs Identify() on two spent e-coins Ψ_1 and Ψ_2 to identify the double-spending perpetrator U. It outputs U's public key pk_U and the double-spending proof Π.

$\{0, 1\} \leftarrow \mathsf{VerifyGuilt}(pk_U, \Pi)$: The double-spending case (pk_U, Π) is publicly verifiable by VerifyGuilt().

Let us recall the core properties of an e-coin scheme:

Correctness. The Withdraw() and Spend() operations terminate successfully with honest participants. An honest recipient accepts an e-coin from a successful Spend().

Balance. No more e-coins can be spent than withdrawn.

Identification of Double-Spenders. Suppose bank B is honest. Let us consider U_1 and U_2 being honest users, each of them receiving the same e-coin during an execution of the Spend() protocol with an adversary, say $\Psi_1 = (s_\Psi, R_1, T_1, \Phi_1)$ and $\Psi_2 = (s_\Psi, R_2, T_2, \Phi_2)$. Then the adversary can be identified by the double-spending detection Identify() with overwhelming probability.

Public Key Recovery. The double-spending detection identifies a perpetrator U by outputting pk_U. We do not require full tracing as proposed in e-cash schemes.

Exculpability. Guilt in double-spending is publicly verifiable.

4   Core Incentive System

We define and analyze the core incentive system based on the preliminaries explained in Sect. 3. We start with definition of the service interface, continue with specification of the security requirements and realization of the system, and we conclude this section with security analysis.

4.1   Service Interface

$()(N_{B,U}) \leftarrow \mathsf{Register}(\sigma_U; sk_U, pk_B)(pk_I)$: A user U registers at bank B anonymously while establishing a bank-specific domain pseudonym $N_{B,U}$ for future transactions.

$(\sigma_\Psi, d_\Psi, s_\Psi)(N_{B,U}) \leftarrow \mathsf{WithdrawIncentive}(\sigma_U; sk_U, pk_B)(sk_B, pk_I)$: A reader U withdraws incentive e-coin from bank B. Reader U outputs a triple of e-coin signature σ_Ψ, double-spend random element d_Ψ and e-coin serial number s_Ψ. Bank B outputs the reader's domain pseudonym $N_{B,U}$.

$()(\Psi, N_{P,U}) \leftarrow \mathsf{SubmitOffer}(\sigma_U, (\sigma_\Psi, d_\Psi, s_\Psi), P; sk_U)(pk_B, pk_I)$: A reader U submits an incentive offer to wiki W, the clearing house. Wiki W outputs a spent e-coin Ψ and the reader's domain pseudonym $N_{P,U}$ for document P. SubmitOffer guarantees reader's proof of possession of the e-coin.

$()(N_{P,R}) \leftarrow$ ProposeReview$(\sigma_R, P, P'; sk_R, pk_I)$(Review$_P; pk_I)$: A reviewer R proposes a review P' for document P anonymously at wiki W. The wiki W outputs the reviewer's domain pseudonym $N_{P,R}$ for document P. It ensures that reviewer R fulfills the entitlement and qualification predicate Review$_P$ and the separation of duties with the author.

$()(N_{P,E}) \leftarrow$ EvaluateReview$(\sigma_E, P, P', result; sk_E, pk_I)(pk_I)$: An editor E rates the review P' for document P with rate $result$. The value $result$ determines approval or rejection. Wiki W enforces the separation of duties.

$(\Psi)(N_{P,R}) \leftarrow$ SubmitReview$(\sigma_R, P, P'; sk_R, pk_B, pk_I)(\sigma_W, (\sigma_\Psi, d_\Psi, s_\Psi); sk_W, pk_I)$: A reviewer R submits an approved review P' to wiki W and obtains the reward incentive e-coin Ψ in return. The domain pseudonym $N_{P,R}$ links the transactions.

$()(\Psi) \leftarrow$ DepositIncentive$(\Psi)()$: A spent e-coin Ψ is sent to bank B.

$(\sigma'_\Psi, d'_\Psi, s'_\Psi)(\Psi) \leftarrow$ ExchangeIncentive$(\Psi, \sigma_W; sk_W, pk_B)(sk_B, pk_I)$: Wiki W deposits a spent e-coin Ψ at bank B in exchange for a fresh e-coin $(\sigma'_\Psi, d'_\Psi, s'_\Psi)$. The bank B receives the deposited e-coin Ψ and may run Identify() to reveal double-spender.

4.2   Requirements

First, to ensure rigorous and impartial reviews, authors, reviewers and editors must benefit from a strong privacy protection. The parties need to be anonymous and their transactions unlinkable between multiple documents.

Second, we consider multiple access control properties. The system must support roles and attributes to qualify reviews. We also allow the certification of a reviewer profession and expertise, which increases trust in reviews and may entitle to claim a larger incentive for an editing task. In addition, the roles of different parties in a review process must be clearly separated. The most common example is that an author may not review and judge her own article.

Third, the system must hold users accountable for their actions to discourage vandalism and fraud. This involves a certification of users' identities, be it by the Wikipedia system itself or trusted third parties, such as government-supported electronic identification issuers. The system supports identity escrow by standard means, for instance, by verifiably encrypting user's true identity to a trusted anonymity revocation authority.

Incentive Security. *Correctness*: The operations terminate successfully with honest participants. *Balance*: No more incentive e-coins can be given than have been withdrawn. *Public Key Recovery*: An adversary can be identified by the double-spending detection with overwhelming probability, the perpetrator U is identified by outputting pk_U. *Exculpability*: Double-spending guilt is publicly verifiable.

Anonymity. The users of the Wikipedia system can be completely anonymous. Users shall be linked only to specific articles by domain pseudonyms.

Unlinkability. Different transactions within a review process, as well as transactions of the entire Wikipedia system are unlinkable. Unlinkability of the underlying technology is orthogonal to this claim (IP addresses, cookies, etc.)

Role- and Attribute-based Entitlement. The system allows role-based (RBAC) and attribute-based access control (ABAC) based on certified identities.

Separation of Duties. The system enforces a separation of conflicting duties (SoD). In particular, an author cannot review or rate her own article.

Accountability. The system holds users accountable for their actions by three means: (i) *Identity Certification*: The users' true identities and roles are certified in anonymous credentials by trusted issuers. (ii) *Master Key Consistency*: All credentials and transactions of a user U are bound to the same identity/master key sk_U. (iii) *Identity Escrow*: We allow a trusted third party to revoke the anonymity of users.

4.3   Realization

We realize the incentive service interface with the abstract primitives from Sect. 3. We focus on protocol diagrams for the complex interactions.

$Register(\sigma_U; sk_U, pk_B)()$: We require each user U to register at bank B and to establish a bank-specific domain pseudonym $N_{B,U}$ in the course of the action. User U proves knowledge of representation of the domain pseudonym $N_{B,U}$ in SPK_1:

$$SPK_1\{(\sigma_U, sk_U, m_1, \ldots, m_l) :$$
$$\mathsf{VerifySig}(\sigma_U, (m_1, \ldots, m_l); pk_I) \land N_{B,U} = (\mathcal{H}(pk_B))^{sk_U}\};$$

$WithdrawIncentive(\sigma_U; sk_U, pk_B)(sk_B, pk_I)$: We require a reader U withdrawing an incentive e-coin to prove her pseudonym $N_{B,U}$ prior to the e-coin withdrawal with SPK_2:

$$SPK_2\{(\sigma_U, sk_U, m_1, \ldots, m_l) :$$
$$\mathsf{VerifySig}(\sigma_U, (m_1, \ldots, m_l); pk_I) \land N_{B,U} = (\mathcal{H}(pk_B))^{sk_U}\};$$

After the reader U successfully logged in as $N_{B,U}$, it engages in a Withdraw() operation with the bank, to obtain the incentive e-coins.

Reader U $(\sigma_U; sk_U, pk_B)$		Bank B (sk_B, pk_I)
$N_{B,U} \leftarrow (\mathcal{H}(pk_B))^{sk_U};$		
$\Phi_2 \leftarrow SPK_2\{\ldots\}$	$\xrightarrow{\quad (N_{B,U}, \Phi_2) \quad}$	Verify: $(N_{B,U}, \Phi_2)$ with pk_I
$(\sigma'_\psi, d_\psi, s_\psi)$	$\xleftarrow{\text{Withdraw}(\sigma_U; sk_U, pk_B)(sk_B, pk_I)}$ ()
$(\sigma_\psi, d_\psi, s_\psi)$		$(N_{B,U})$

$SubmitOffer(\sigma_U, (\sigma_\psi, d_\psi, s_\psi), P; sk_U)(pk_B)$: To submit an offer, a reader U spends an incentive e-coin with the wiki W and proves knowledge of representation of his domain pseudonym $N_{P,U}$ for a document P by SPK_3:

$$SPK_3\{(sk_U, d_\psi, R) : \qquad T = g_B^{sk_U R} g_B^{d_\psi} \land N_{P,U} = (\mathcal{H}(P))^{sk_U}\};$$

Reader U $(\sigma_U, (\sigma_\Psi, d_\Psi, s_\Psi), P; sk_U)$		Wiki W (pk_B, pk_I)

$N_{P,U} \leftarrow (\mathcal{H}(P))^{sk_U};$

$$(T,R) \xleftarrow{\quad \text{Spend}(\sigma_U, (\sigma_\Psi, d_\Psi, s_\Psi); sk_U)(pk_B, pk_I);\quad} (\Psi)$$

$$\Phi_3 \leftarrow SPK_3\{\ldots\} \xrightarrow{\quad (N_{P,U}, \Phi_3) \quad} \text{Verify: } (N_{B,U}, \Phi_3) \text{ with } pk_I$$

()		$(\Psi, N_{P,U})$

ProposeReview$(\sigma_R, P, P'; sk_R, pk_I)(\text{Review}_P; pk_I)$: A reviewer R may propose a review P' for document P by proving knowledge of representation of domain pseudonym $N_{P,R}$ to wiki W. SPK_4 proves in addition that the reviewer R certificate σ_R fulfills the predicate Review$_P$, e.g., that reviewer R is a doctor:

$$SPK_4\{(\sigma_R, sk_R, m_1, \ldots, m_l):$$
$$\text{VerifySigPred}(\sigma_R, (m_1, \ldots, m_l), \text{Review}_P; pk_I) \wedge N_{P,R} = (\mathcal{H}(P))^{sk_R}\};$$

The wiki W verifies that the reviewer R is different from the author of the document P by comparing their domain pseudonyms.

EvaluateReview$(\sigma_E, P, P', result; sk_E, pk_I)(pk_I)$: An editor E can evaluate a review P' after having proven knowledge of representation of his domain pseudonym $N_{P,E}$ in SPK_5:

$$SPK_5\{(\sigma_E, sk_E, m_1, \ldots, m_l):$$
$$\text{VerifySig}(\sigma_E, (m_1, \ldots, m_l); pk_I) \wedge N_{P,E} = (\mathcal{H}(P))^{sk_E}\}(result);$$

The wiki W verifies that editor E and reviewer R are different by comparing their domain pseudonyms.

SubmitReview$(\sigma_R, P, P'; sk_R, pk_B, pk_I)(\sigma_W, (\sigma_\Psi, d_\Psi, s_\Psi); sk_W, pk_I)$: When a reviewer R submits an approved review P', she needs to prove knowledge of representation of her domain pseudonym $N_{P,R}$ first to link the transaction to the previous ones:

$$SPK_6\{(\sigma_R, sk_R, m_1, \ldots, m_l):$$
$$\text{VerifySig}(\sigma_R, (m_1, \ldots, m_l); pk_I) \wedge N_{P,R} = (\mathcal{H}(P))^{sk_R}\};$$

The wiki W only engages in the Spend() protocol with reviewer R after successful proof. The reviewer R obtains an incentive e-coin Ψ and can subsequently deposit it at the bank B.

Reviewer R $(\sigma_R, P, P'; sk_R, pk_B, pk_I)$		Wiki W $(\sigma_W, (\sigma_\Psi, d_\Psi, s_\Psi); sk_W, pk_I)$

$N_{P,R} \leftarrow (\mathcal{H}(P))^{sk_R};$

$$\Phi_6 \leftarrow SPK_6\{\ldots\} \xrightarrow{\quad (N_{P,R}, \Phi_6) \quad} \text{Verify: } (N_{P,R}, \Phi_6) \text{ with } pk_I$$

$$(\Psi) \xleftarrow{\quad \text{Spend}(\sigma_W, (\sigma_\Psi, d_\Psi, s_\Psi); sk_W)(pk_B) \quad} (T,R)$$

(Ψ)		$(N_{P,R})$

4.4   Security Analysis

Incentive Security. The balance property of the e-cash system directly transfers to the incentive balance of our construction. The e-cash system's Identify() and VerifyGuilt() operations on user public keys enforce *Balance* and *Exculpability* properties.

Anonymity and Unlinkability. We based our construction on anonymous credentials as root identity. Throughout the system's transactions, users only prove knowledge of representation of their domain pseudonyms and their actual identities are kept confidential, except in the case of double-spending.

The cross-document unlinkability is maintained because the domain pseudonyms are uniformly distributed random group elements under the assumption of the random oracle model (ROM). The decision whether two keys, x and y, are equal given $(\mathcal{H}(P))^x, \mathcal{H}(Q))^y, P, Q)$ is hard under the Decision Diffie-Hellman (DDH) assumption in the ROM. We break the linking of non-transferable e-coins by an exchange between clearing house and bank via the ExchangeIncentive() operation.

Role- and Attribute-based Entitlement. We use the certified attributes in user's identity credential σ_U as flexible entitlement mechanism. Our system supports RBAC by certified role attributes, as well as ABAC by selective disclosure of further attributes. We employ this technique in the ProposeReview() operation: a reviewer R proves that her identity credential σ_R fulfills a review predicate Review$_P$. It applies to all of the proofs of representation of domain pseudonyms.

Separation of Duties. The separation of duties is enforced by proofs over domain pseudonyms. We realize *subject-based* separation of duties, the editor of the document is different from the author, by an inequality check of the domain pseudonyms. We realize *role-based* separation of duties, the document can only be confirmed under four-eyes principle, where one user has the role of a *Clerk* and another has the role of a *Manager*, by signature proofs of knowledge of roles and attributes associated with a domain pseudonym. The probability that two keys, x and y, for which $(\mathcal{H}(P))^x, \mathcal{H}(P))^y)$ collide is negligible as both are uniformly distributed random group elements given the ROM.

Accountability. We get *Identity Certification* and *Master Key Consistency* properties by design of the anonymous credential system. We achieve the *Identity Escrow* property by including a Verifiable Encryption (e.g., Camenisch and Shoup [10]) of a user's true identity sk_U towards a trusted third party. We consider this procedure a standard technique and do not elaborate on it.

5   Functional Extensions and Future Work

Although we implemented the core incentive system as elaborated in Sect. 6, we have not yet realized certain extension ideas. The following explains possible extensions for rating reviews on contributions and building reviewer's reputation.

Rating Reviews. In the presented system, the wiki W is responsible for checking the quality of the reviews and, if it finds the quality sufficient, for releasing spent incentive e-coins to the reviewer R. Alternatively, one could let the wiki community rate these reviews and have the wiki W only release the e-coins to the reviewer R, if the submitted review obtained a sufficiently high ranking. The mechanism would proceed as follows: Users (raters) sign their rating of the review with their domain pseudonym. The wiki W collects these ratings, checks that the domain pseudonyms of the raters and of the reviewer are different (separation of duties), as well as that each domain pseudonym of a rater only occurs once (one-time rating).

If there are several reviews, the offered e-coins can be distributed to different reviewers in proportion of the reviews ranking. This approach encourages reviewers to provide quality reviews in order to gain a high ranking and collect most of the e-coins. At the same time, it prevents reviewers from collecting all of the e-coins for poor quality reviews.

Reviewer Reputation. Rating of a review provides feedback on the quality of the review. This naturally lends itself to be used for an (anonymous) reputation system. Thus, the wiki W could issue reputation credentials (points) to reviewers and authors based on the quality of the reviews and articles. Articles could be ranked by users similarly to the reviews as described above.

More precisely, a reputation system can be implemented as follows. In addition to earned incentives, the wiki W could also issue an anonymous one-time credential to the user U (reviewer or author) according to the received average rating. This credential can be realized with the e-coin scheme, where the rating is encoded in the denomination. One either uses a different bank public key for each denomination or one extends the e-cash scheme to include denomination as an e-coin attribute. These *reputation e-coins* can then be gathered by the author or reviewers.

Let us assume some reputation authority that issues credentials which state user's reputation. Users can then exchange the reputation e-coins with the reputation authority against an updated reputation credential without this transaction being linkable to the corresponding article/review. The one-time spending property of the e-coin will ensure that each rating can be used only once. Depending on how the reputation is computed, the rating e-coin and the old reputation credential cannot be exchanged directly for a new reputation credential, but the user U might need to have a pseudonymous account where he can deposit all the different ratings and then get an updated reputation credential issued once this computation is done. We leave a detailed discussion to the extended version of this paper.

6   Example Application

Wikipedia is a large-scale online encyclopedia project that at this time has grown to $\sim 3.35 \cdot 10^6$ articles in the English version and $\sim 9.25 \cdot 10^6$ articles in total [27], and that is beginning to rival more established compendiums of human knowledge [16]. Its software platform, MediaWiki, allows anybody with Internet access to read and edit shared articles. The most important criteria in Wikipedia's search for new quality assessment methods are the immediacy typical for social media as well as accuracy, which can be challenging [24].

The German Wikipedia chapter has deployed one such process in the form of the MediaWiki extension FlaggedRevs [13]. It allows eligible users, e.g., those who have earned editor role by being active community member for a certain duration, to review articles. In one configuration, review criteria include levels of accuracy, depth, and readability, and the review status is prominently displayed along with each article as important quality indication. According to the FlaggedRevs 2008 report [15], approximately 90.8% of the German Wikipedia articles have been reviewed at least once, even though, mostly by small pockets of active (expert) contributors.

Our example application functions as an extension to the FlaggedRevs extension and is registered as add-on PHP functionality in the MediaWiki. We register several incentive handling functions at its main code entry points. If both extensions, FlaggedRevs and Mango are installed, users can offer incentives when they want certain articles to be reviewed, and reviewers can earn these incentives by providing their expert insights through the revision process.

We report that we have implemented the presented incentive system architecture in the MediaWiki (see Fig. 2) as the Mango extension, as well as the cryptographic incentives system from Sect. 2 using the Identity Mixer library [17] based on the SRSA. The MediaWiki extension Mango contains the appropriate hooks to accommodate the cryptographic functions and serves as a glue between MediaWiki and the incentives system.

6.1 System Architecture

Static Design. Figure 1 shows the same entities as defined in Sect. 2 and concentrates on the software architecture of components that allow humans to participate in the scheme. High-level components have been realized as Java servlets.

Each user-facing component has an id, a password (corresponding to its MediaWiki account information) and a pair of cryptographic keys (for participating in the protocols). The bank B and the clearing W are special in that certain other components must have knowledge of these entities' public keys and network addresses in their configurations.

The components marked as *user* and *reviewer* correspond to U and R as defined in Sect. 2, and they receive communication at anonymous network addresses $addr_U$ and $addr_R$ respectively. The component marked as *clearing* corresponds to W, it receives communication at address $addr_W$. The clearing W functions as a front-end to MediaWiki and its extensions, thus linking its core logic (implemented in PHP and JavaScript by the MediaWiki conventions) to privacy-friendly incentives system (implemented in Java). The component marked *bank* corresponds to B and it receives communication at address $addr_B$.

All entity components maintain relational databases (cylinder shapes in Fig. 1) locally. The architecture does not assume that their private data is stored at any central location. For all indicated mappings, $a \mapsto b$ serves as a shorthand notation for the mapping from the set of all possible values for a to the set of all possible values for b.

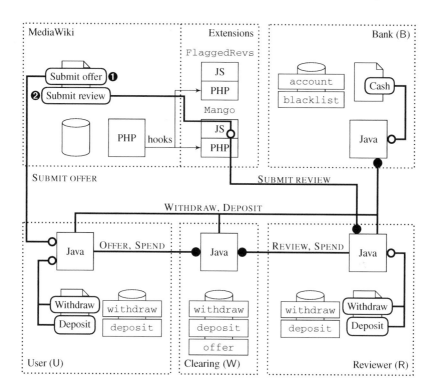

Fig. 1. System architecture

Each bank B maintains two tables: The table `account` is a mapping $N_{B,U} \mapsto (pk_U, n)$, where $N_{B,U}$ is a domain pseudonym computed by user U using address of the bank and n is the current balance of user U's account at the bank. The table `blacklist` is a mapping $N_{B,U} \mapsto \{ x_j \}_j$, where x_j are textual log entries pertaining to past double-spending behavior by user U, including the proof of double spending which can be verified by other parties.

Each user U maintains two tables: The table `withdraw` is a set of e-coins $\{ \Psi_i \}_i$ that were withdrawn from a bank B and have not yet been spent. The table `deposit` is a set of spent e-coins $\{ \Omega_i \}_i$ that have been received from another party, but have not yet been deposited at a bank B.

The clearing W is an extension of the user component and maintains one additional table: The table `offer` is a mapping $P \times N_{P,U} \mapsto (n)$ where $N_{P,U}$ is the reader U's domain pseudonym for article P and n is the number of e-coins offered for a review of the article P.

Dynamic Design. We will now explain the dynamic aspects of the system by following two representative use cases. The WITHDRAW, SPEND and DEPOSIT serve as high-level protocols calling the core incentive system's interface introduced in Sect. 4. In the first use case a user U offers privacy-friendly incentive points for an article review. The flow for this use case starts at the points marked ❶ in Fig. 1 (a user U presses the

"Submit offer" button). Our walk-through assumes that an eligible user U has already logged into MediaWiki and that the system is in the right state. We present an elaborate version of this flow in the extended version of this paper.

Step 1.1 To offer e-coins for a non-stable (not reviewed) article, user U fills in an HTML form (see Fig. 2(a)) and presses the "Submit offer" button.

Step 1.2 The web browser submits user's request to the user U component, which runs locally on the user's machine as a Java servlet. The component U checks its `withdraw` table if sufficient number of unspent e-coins is available. In case of insufficient number of unspent e-coins, the component U will contact the bank B with user's consent, withdraw additional e-coins executing the WITHDRAW protocol and continue with submitting the offer.

Step 1.3 The user U and the clearing W components interact in the SUBMIT OFFER request to spend an incentive e-coin.

Step 1.4 The clearing W receives the e-coins, deposits them to the bank B, withdraws fresh unspent e-coins and stores them in its table `withdraw`. Identification of the article to which the offer pertains along with the number of e-coins offered are stored in the table `offer`.

In the second use case a reviewer R receives privacy-friendly incentive points after conducting a review. The flow for this use case starts at the points marked ❷ in Fig. 1 (a reviewer R presses the button "Submit review"). Our walk-through assumes that an eligible reviewer R has already logged into MediaWiki and that the system is in the right state.

Step 2.1 A reviewer R chooses to submit a review. To do so, she fills in an HTML form (see Fig. 2(b)) and presses the "Submit review" button.

Step 2.2 This results in contacting the Java servlet of the reviewer R and an invocation of the clearing W involving both JavaScript and PHP.

Step 2.3 The clearing W looks up the entry in the table `offer`. On success, it spends the incentive e-coins with reviewer R using the SPEND protocol and it deletes the corresponding entries from `offer`.

Step 2.4 The reviewer R receives the spent e-coins and interacts with the bank B to exchange the e-coins for unspent ones (by executing DEPOSIT, then WITHDRAW) and stores the fresh e-coins in its table `withdraw`.

(a) Offering incentives.   (b) Earning incentives.

Fig. 2. Our privacy-friendly incentives realization in use

6.2 Anonymous and Pseudonymous Use

We note that MediaWiki already supports *pseudonymous use*. While this already affords relatively good privacy properties, our privacy-friendly incentive system from Sect. 2 can be extended to allow fully anonymous access to Wikipedia. In order to achieve this, the access control of MediaWiki needs to be adjusted to use domain pseudonym of a user and a proof that the user registered properly, the MediaWiki extension from [22] can be used to achieve this. We discuss the actual linkability in the MediaWiki system in the extended version of this paper.

7 Related Work

Incentives are useful to create reputation systems. Steinbrecher studied privacy-protecting reputation systems [23] using pseudonyms. In such pseudonymous solutions, the transactions that are taken into account to build reputation can all be linked together. Therefore, many authors have claimed that achieving privacy in reputation systems is impossible [20]. In contrast, in our scheme one can build reputation from different transactions without these being linkable.

Adler and de Alfaro [1] proposed an orthogonal content-driven trust extension for MediaWiki, called WikiTrust. They focus on the analysis of a document's author, her reputation, origin, and trust, whereas our system considers the users' interactions in a double-blind review system. Lysyanskaya and co-authors [5] proposed and implemented an incentive system based on plain e-cash and fair exchange or file sharing applications. Their work focuses on the (fair) exchange of token and digital items. Androulaki and co-authors [3] proposed a reputation scheme for a pseudonymous peer-to-peer network. Their scheme uses e-cash to realize reputation points offered after a transaction is executed between network participants.

In contrast, we are interested in the (anonymous) relationships of the parties using e-cash to realize incentive points to enhance the quality of content. Furthermore, we propose possible extensions to our system to realize reputations of participating parties.

8 Conclusion

This paper has introduced novel concept of a privacy-friendly incentive system to rate user-generated content. We have proposed the first realization of such a system that draws on ideas from e-cash and anonymous credentials. The presented solution is privacy-friendly both from a theoretical and an applied perspective. In addition, we have contributed a practical architecture that integrates well with the open-source collaboration platform MediaWiki. To this end, we have extended MediaWiki for semi-anonymous use in a prototype environment, and designed the architecture such that it can support anonymous use by later adding anonymous credentials for authentication.

We report that we have implemented the cryptographic incentive system on top of the Identity Mixer library [7,17]. We have realized a MediaWiki extension `Mango` with appropriate hooks for the cryptographic protocols and we integrated both results into

MediaWiki, that is, hooking the implementation of the cryptographic protocols into the MediaWiki plug-ins.

We believe that providing such an incentive system nurtures high-quality content on electronic collaboration platforms by vigorous user interaction and rigorous double-blind reviews. We hope for a raise in quality and trustworthiness of user-generated content, in particular, if earned incentive points can be exchanged (at a suitable exchange rate) for real goods, such as CDs or vouchers.

Finally, note that our solution can be extended in multiple ways, most prominently through: (i) multifaceted incentives, (ii) transferable e-cash, (iii) identity escrow, and (iv) complex roles and policies.

Acknowledgment

This work has been funded by the European Community's Seventh Framework Programme (FP7/2007-2013) under grant agreement no. 216483.

References

1. Adler, B.T., de Alfaro, L.: A content-driven reputation system for the Wikipedia. In: Proceedings of the 16th International Conference on World Wide Web, pp. 261–270. ACM Press, New York (2007)
2. von Ahn, L.: Games with a Purpose. IEEE Computer Magazine (June 2006)
3. Androulaki, E., Choi, S.G., Bellovin, S.M., Malkin, T.: Reputation systems for anonymous networks. In: Borisov, N., Goldberg, I. (eds.) PETS 2008. LNCS, vol. 5134, pp. 202–218. Springer, Heidelberg (2008)
4. Bangerter, E., Camenisch, J., Lysyanskaya, A.: A cryptographic framework for the controlled release of certified data. In: Christianson, B., Crispo, B., Malcolm, J.A., Roe, M. (eds.) Security Protocols 2004. LNCS, vol. 3957, pp. 20–42. Springer, Heidelberg (2006)
5. Belenkiy, M., Chase, M., Erway, C.C., Jannotti, J., Küpçü, A., Lysyanskaya, A.: Incentivizing outsourced computation. In: NetEcon, pp. 85–90 (2008)
6. Camenisch, J., Groß, T., Hladky, P., Hoertnagl, C.: Privacy-friendly incentives and their application to Wikipedia (extended version). Cryptology ePrint Archive Report 2010/401, IACR (July 2010), http://eprint.iacr.org/2010/401
7. Camenisch, J., Herreweghen, E.V.: Design and implementation of the *idemix* anonymous credential system. In: Proc. 9th ACM Conference on Computer and Communications Security. ACM Press, New York (2002)
8. Camenisch, J., Hohenberger, S., Lysyanskaya, A.: Compact E-cash. In: Cramer, R. (ed.) EUROCRYPT 2005. LNCS, vol. 3494, pp. 302–321. Springer, Heidelberg (2005)
9. Camenisch, J., Kiayias, A., Yung, M.: On the portability of generalized schnorr proofs. In: Joux, A. (ed.) Advances in Cryptology — EUROCRYPT 2009. LNCS, vol. 5479, pp. 425–442. Springer, Heidelberg (2009)
10. Camenisch, J., Shoup, V.: Practical verifiable encryption and decryption of discrete logarithms. In: Boneh, D. (ed.) CRYPTO 2003. LNCS, vol. 2729, pp. 126–144. Springer, Heidelberg (2003)
11. Camenisch, J., Stadler, M.: Efficient group signature schemes for large groups. In: Kaliski, B. (ed.) CRYPTO 1997. LNCS, vol. 1294, pp. 410–424. Springer, Heidelberg (1997)

12. Damgård, I., Fujisaki, E.: An integer commitment scheme based on groups with hidden order. In: Zheng, Y. (ed.) ASIACRYPT 2002. LNCS, vol. 2501, pp. 125–142. Springer, Heidelberg (2002)
13. Extension: FlaggedRevs, http://www.mediawiki.org/wiki/Extension:FlaggedRevs
14. Fiat, A., Shamir, A.: How to prove yourself: Practical solutions to identification and signature problems. In: Odlyzko, A.M. (ed.) CRYPTO 1986. LNCS, vol. 263, pp. 186–194. Springer, Heidelberg (1987)
15. Flaggedrevs report december 2008 (December 2008), http://meta.wikimedia.org/wiki/FlaggedRevs_Report_December_2008
16. Giles, J.: Internet encyclopaedias go head to head. Nature 438 (December 14, 2005), http://www.nature.com/nature/journal/v438/n7070/full/438900a.html
17. IBM: Cryptographic protocols of the Identity Mixer library, v. 2.3. IBM Research Report RZ3730, IBM Research (2010), http://domino.research.ibm.com/library/cyberdig.nsf/index.html
18. Lampe, C., Resnick, P.: Slash(dot) and burn: Distributed moderation in a large online conversation space. In: ACM CHI 2004 Conference on Human Factors in Computing Systems (2004)
19. Lysyanskaya, A., Rivest, R., Sahai, A., Wolf, S.: Pseudonym systems. In: Heys, H., Adams, C. (eds.) SAC 1999. LNCS, vol. 1758, p. 184. Springer, Heidelberg (2000)
20. Pavlov, E., Rosenschein, J.S., Topol, Z.: Supporting privacy in decentralized additive reputation systems. In: Jensen, C., Poslad, S., Dimitrakos, T. (eds.) iTrust 2004. LNCS, vol. 2995, pp. 108–119. Springer, Heidelberg (2004)
21. Pedersen, T.P.: Non-interactive and information-theoretic secure verifiable secret sharing. In: Feigenbaum, J. (ed.) CRYPTO 1991. LNCS, vol. 576, pp. 129–140. Springer, Heidelberg (1992)
22. PrimeLife project, http://www.primelife.eu
23. Steinbrecher, S.: Design options for privacy-respecting reputation systems within centralised internet communities. In: SEC, pp. 123–134 (2006)
24. Viégas, F.B., Wattenberg, M., Dave, K.: Studying cooperation and conflict between authors with history flow visualizations. In: Proceedings of the 2004 Conference on Human Factors in Computing Systems, CHI 2004 (2004)
25. A little sleuthing unmasks writer of Wikipedia prank (December 2005), http://www.nytimes.com/2005/12/11/business/media/11web.html
26. Wikipedia to limit changes to articles on people (August 2009), http://www.nytimes.com/2009/08/25/technology/internet/25wikipedia.html
27. Wikipedia: Size comparisons (August 2010), http://en.wikipedia.org/wiki/Wikipedia:Size_comparisons

Policy Provisioning for Distributed Identity Management Systems

Hidehito Gomi

Yahoo! JAPAN Research, 9-7-1 Akasaka, Minato-ku, Tokyo 107-6211, Japan
hgomi@yahoo-corp.jp

Abstract. A policy provisioning framework is described that supports the management of the lifecycle of identity information distributed beyond security domains. A model for creating data handling policies reflecting the intentions of its system administrator and the privacy preferences of the data owner is explained. Also, algorithms for systematically integrating data handling policies from system entities in different administrative domains are presented. This framework enables data handling policies to be properly deployed and enforced in a way that enhances security and privacy.

1 Introduction

Many applications are being executed in distributed systems and among multiple different organizations with the ongoing development of the Internet. Personal information in such environments is often exchanged beyond the boundaries of security domains. It is generally difficult for both administrators and owners to control data once they are propagated outside their security domains. Thus, identity management in distributed environments is one of the most important issues in preserving security and privacy.

There have been several technical projects on identity management including access control and privacy management. Privacy-aware access control [1, 2] has especially aimed at incorporating privacy-related policies into traditional access control policies. Another emerging concept of *identity governance* [3] has addressed user-centric control of access and introduced a method of tracking data for propagating identity information. Although these research efforts have enabled fine-grained access control for managing identity from security and privacy perspectives, they have not fully addressed how data handling policies can be created and integrated, which satisfy the different requirements of distinct actors in different security domains from a practical viewpoint. Since these actors are involved with data practices, but generally have different responsibilities, the enforcing policies need to be created from administrative and privacy standpoints.

This paper proposes a policy provisioning framework that helps to manage the lifecycle of identity information using handling polices that reflect its system administrator's intentions and its data owner's preferences from both administrative and privacy viewpoints. Also described are algorithms that enable data

E. de Leeuw, S. Fischer-Hübner, L. Fritsch (Eds.): IDMAN 2010, IFIP AICT 343, pp. 130–144, 2010.

handling policies or privacy preferences to be created and integrated from multiple actors to control access to identity information. This work focuses on collaboratively building a policy provisioning model and framework for distributed identity management systems, whereas the representation of policies and detailed resolutions on policy conflicts are beyond the scope of this work.

The rest of this paper is organized as follows. Section 2 presents related work and Section 3 introduces a policy provisioning model. Section 4 describes a policy provisioning framework based on the proposed model. Section 5 discusses several issues related to policy management and Section 6 concludes the paper with a summary of the key points and an outline of future work.

2   Related Work

This section highlight research efforts in the area of access control, privacy management, and policy specification languages related to the work presented in this paper.

The idea of controlling access to data even after they have been disseminated has been considered especially by the digital rights management (DRM) community [4, 5]. Their work has focused on protecting digital content from unauthorized copying and distribution by disseminating packages containing the content data and access control policies. Several efforts [6, 7] toward managing privacy have introduced the concept of "sticky policies", in which handling policies are directly associated with personal information. In their approaches, users retain control over their personal information even after it has been disclosed by enforcing its privacy policies, which reflect their preferences about how it is to be used next at its recipient site. The work here inherits the basic idea of tight bundling of data and policy described above, regardless of whether the type of policy is security or privacy related.

There have been numerous research efforts related to extensions of traditional mechanisms for access control to protect privacy [1, 2]. Ardagna et al. [2] proposed a privacy-aware system to control access that enforced access control policies together with privacy policies such as release and data handling policies that regulated the use of personal information in secondary applications. They focused on the introduction of data handling policy language and the integration of traditional access control and data handling policies created from two actors, i.e., a service provider that managed personal information and a user who originally had the information. However, their work did not describe how data handling policies were created and deployed in a system that consisted of entities that had distinct responsibilities or roles and that supported multiple chains to disseminate data among those entities. The work described here instead focuses on policy management in which a data managing provider collaboratively establishes data enforcing policies.

Other relevant work on privacy management has been identity governance, which is an emerging concept to provide fine-grained conditional disclosure of identity information and enforce corresponding data handling policies. Liberty

Alliance specifies fundamental privacy constraints on such governance as the use, display, retention, storage, and propagation of identity information [8]. Gomi [3] introduced privacy-aware tracking policies and a data mechanism for monitoring the status of a user's identity information and enforcing its privacy policies to regulate its secondary use after it had been disseminated. Although theses allow access control that enhances privacy by defining new types of expressive privacy policies, they do not fully take into consideration the integration or composition of polices among distinct actors located in different administrative domains. The proposed framework addresses a method of transmitting and incorporating data handling policies associated with shared identity information between actors.

There has been a great deal of work on description languages and constraints for privacy policies. P3P [9] and its complement APPEL [10] provide the means for expressing comprehensive user preferences. XACML [11] specifies an access control language to describe access control constraints and provides privacy extensions to support privacy related constraints. EPAL [12] provides a privacy policy language for governing data practices in enterprise systems. The Liberty Identity Governance Framework (IGF) [8] specifies privacy constraints. Although the framework proposed here assumes such an expressive privacy policy and access control language as basic building blocks, it focuses on managing the lifecycles within which security and privacy policies are enforced irrespective of their schema or the format they are represented in.

Relevant work has been done in the field of policy management such as policy integration and conflict resolution. Mazzoleni et al. [13] proposed policy integration algorithms for XACML. They believed that XACML had not been built to manage security for systems in which enterprises were dynamically constructed with the collaboration of multiple independent subjects. The approach proposed here is relevant in that entities located in different security domains collaboratively share data and their policies. Belokosztolszki and Moody [14] introduced meta-policies for distributed Role-Based Access Control (RBAC). They found it difficult to specify a policy that would not conflict with local requirements. Their work is relevant in that they considered a hierarchical structure for managing policy in distributed systems. Bettini et al. [15] formalized a rule-based policy framework that controlled access by user requests for action by evaluating rules associated with provisions and obligations, which were pre-conditions to be satisfied before and post-conditions to be satisfied after the action was performed. Their framework provided a mechanism for reasoning about the policy rules in the presence of provisions and obligations in a single administrative domain to derive an appropriate set of these. In contrast, the framework presented here composes a set of policies using different actors with different responsibilities in distinct domains and it enforces the composed policies reflecting a system administrator and a user in distributed identity management systems.

3   Model

This section explains a model for policy provisioning.

A **data subject (DS)** is an individual to whom personal data is related. A DS delegates the secure management and convenient utilization of his or her personal data to other entities specifying privacy preferences on how the data is to be handled by them. A DS can demonstrate his or her wishes by means of *consent* to questions from other entities as one of representations of privacy preferences.

A **data controller (DC)** is an entity that maintains DSs' personal data on his or her behalf in compliance with its own privacy or security policies reflecting both their privacy preferences. A DC can securely provide a DS's personal data to another entity in a different administrative domain on the basis of the agreement with the entity on how the data are to be used and handled. A DC is liable for securely managing and propagating a DS's personal data.

A **data processor (DP)** is an entity that processes a DS's personal data obtained from a DC in conformity with the agreement reached with the latter on how the data are to be handled. A DP is placed in a distinct administrative domain from that of a DC. A DP is liable for handling personal data originally managed by a DC. This liability is different from that for a DC since a DP does not need to maintain or determine the purposes for which the data are processed, and since this liability depends on the agreement on data processing between a DC and a DP.

The DC and DP are not actual entities; they are simply roles in the model. Therefore, a single entity can play both roles. That is, when entity e_1 acting as a DP receives personal data from entity e_2 acting as a DC with an agreed upon policy allowing e_1 to store and further propagate the received data to the other entity, e_3, e_1 can act as a DC for e_3. In other words, the relationship between DC and DP is relative and one-way specific to the pair of two entities for the particular types of personal data in this model. In this example, e_1 can be a DC for e_3, but cannot be a DC for e_2, because e_2 was originally a DC for e_1.

It is assumed that these entities are trusted and can be expected to comply with the agreement. The purpose of this work was to establish an agreement on data handling between trusted entities and create and deploy policies to be appropriately enforced, rather than to detect their misbehaviors.

3.1   Policy Binding to Data

Data and their handling policies in this model are tightly associated. When a DC receives an access request to data, the DC determines whether to grant or deny the access enforcing the handling policies associated with the data. When a DP attempts to process data, the DP also uses the handling policies associated with the data to make an authorization decision on the data processing.

If a DC needs to provide a DP with personal data, the DC encapsulates the data and their associated policies and transfers both to the DP. The DP complies with the policy agreed upon and received from the DC prior to receiving the data. Namely, agreed upon policies migrate with the data to govern the data practices of a DC that receives both the data and policies. The agreed upon policies

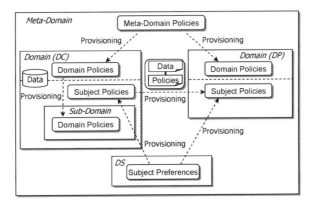

Fig. 1. Hierarchical Policy Model

correspond to an agreement between a DC and a DP when data are transferred and are the legal grounds for appropriately restricting data processing by a DP.

The encapsulation and transport mechanisms of data and policies are beyond the scope of this model. Instead, it focuses on the design of the framework for hierarchically developing policies among distinct entities, which will be described in the next section.

3.2   Policy Hierarchy

Figure 1 outlines a hierarchical policy model that encompasses the defined entities and exchanged policies.

The *Meta-Domain* is a meta-organization or system such as an industrial department or a governmental body to which the *Domains* belong. The Domain is an administrative organization or system independent of others that acts as DC or DP entities. A meta-domain and a domain have a relative association. The *Sub-Domain* belongs to its upper class domain. The relationships between the Meta-Domain and Domain, and Domain and Sub-Domain are hierarchical. These relationships generally hold true without limiting the representation in Fig. 1. A domain acting as a DC provides a DS with a service that manages the DS's personal data. A domain acting as a DP provides a DS with a service that uses a DS's personal data.

A meta-domain has *Meta-Domain Policies* that are meta-level and general policies constraining the activities of all domains that belong to the meta-domain, by reflecting its laws or regulations with which the domains need to comply.

Domain Policies are organizational domain-specific policies that inherit the meta-domain policies in the meta-domain, and are not specific to DSs. When a DC propagates personal data to a DP, the DC and the DP agree on a set of policies on how the data are to be used and handled prior to being propagated. The agreed upon policies migrate with the data from the DC to the DP.

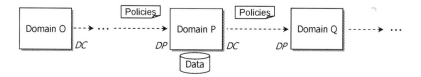

Fig. 2. Policy Provisioning Chain

Subject Policies are specified by a domain for a DS, reflecting *Subject Prefer-ences*, which are a DS's privacy-related preferences for handling the DS's personal data. As a result of incorporating subject preferences into subject policies, a DS needs to follow the subject policies specified by domains to enjoy their services. More detailed descriptions on how these policies are created and provided will be given in the sections that follow.

3.3   Policy Provisioning Chain

A DS's data possibly propagates from domain to domain. Here, the data handling policies associated with the data also propagate from a domain acting as a DC to a domain acting as a DP. The flow of the policies constitutes a chain of domains as seen in Fig. 2.

When domain P manages data, it obtains meta-domain policies from its meta-domain, and additionally agreed upon policies if the data have originally been propagated by another domain acting as a DC to incorporate them into its domain policies. P, acting as a DC, propagates the data and their handling policies to domain Q, acting as a DP, after P and Q have agreed upon the policies. As a result of data being propagated and policies being agreed on, Q becomes responsible for handling the data. In this way, if data propagate from domain to domain, their associated handling policies change to ones reflecting local domain policies and propagate together with data for enforcing the behavior of another domain receiving the data. The first entity that provides policies in a provisioning chain is called the *Root Domain*, which is denoted by domain O in Fig. 2.

There are two types of relationships between adjacent domains in the policy provisioning chain. The first is a hierarchical relationship. In this case, since the upper domain manages the lower domain in a policy hierarchy, the lower domain inherits the policies from those of the upper domain. The second is a propagation relationship in different domains that are placed on the same level in the policy hierarchy. Here, policies are propagated from a DC to a DP after they reach agreement on how data are to be handled.

3.4   Policy Components

This model has several components related to policies, which are relevant to the ones defined in XACML.

- *Action.* An action is a specific activity that invokes a function call or sends a request to other domains.
- *Data.* Data represents a subject's personal data identified by its data type.
- *Rule.* A rule is the basic element of a policy.
- *Policy.* A policy is a combination of one or more rules.
- *Policy set.* A policy set is a collection of one or more policies.

Policies are represented in the following sections in declarative form irrespective of the language or format for coding policies.

4   Policy Provisioning Framework

This section explains detailed procedures on managing the lifecycle of policies as well as on the data to be managed using the policies.

4.1   Policy Creation

Meta-Domain Policy Creation. Meta-domain policies are created by the administrator of the domain. Since a root domain corresponds to an administrative organization such as an industrial company or governmental body, its meta-policies are created from the administrative viewpoints of privacy protection laws or cooperate compliance.

There are two types of meta-domain policies, i.e., *common policies* and *governance policies*. Common policies are general and do not specify concrete constraints in them such as data types, subjects, and context. For example, a meta-domain policy statement in a natural language is "No entities must propagate personal data owned by subjects to other subjects and domains without their consent." This statement can be specified in the following declarative form:

$$(\text{P0.a}) : \neg doable(a) \Leftarrow subject(u_1) \wedge subject(u_2) \wedge own(u_1, data)$$
$$\wedge \ action(send(u_1, u_2, data), a) \wedge \neg consent(u_1, a).$$

In the above representation, operators $\neg$, $\wedge$, and $\Leftarrow$ respectively specify logical negation, conjunction, and reverse implication. Axiom $doable(\cdot)$ indicates that a specified action is allowed to be executed if all the constraints specified after operator $\Leftarrow$ are satisfied. $subject(u)$ means that u is a DS in this domain. In $action(send(u_1, u_2, data), a)$, action a is defined as an action where DS u_1 propagates $data$ to DS u_2. Axioms $own(u_1, data)$ and $consent(u_1, a)$ respectively indicate that u_1 owns $data$ and that u_1 consents to the execution of action a.

Governance policies are meta-level and directive ones for managing the privileges and behavior of sub-domains. For example, information on personal attributes such as name and address can ultimately be managed by the DS that owns them, assuming the concept is acceptable from the viewpoint of local laws.

$$(\text{P0.b}) : doable(a) \Leftarrow subject(u) \wedge own(u, att) \wedge action(manage(u, att), a)$$
$$\wedge \ attributes(att, name) \wedge attributes(att, address).$$

In the form above, att denotes personal attributes and $attributes(att, type)$ indicates that att includes data type $type$. Axiom $action(manage(u, att), a)$ denotes that action a is defined as a set of actions for managing att including "read" and "write" actions. Here, DS u has privileges to manage his or her own name and address.

In contrast, a digital content owner can state that no subscribers have any right to propagate the content in the following form, which has been used as an example:

$$(P0.c) : \neg doable(a) \Leftarrow subject(u_1) \wedge subscriber(u_2) \wedge \neg subscriber(u_3)$$
$$\wedge\ own(u_1, cont) \wedge action(send(u_2, u_3, cont), a),$$

where $subscriber(u)$ denotes a subscriber of the digital content. $own(u_1, cont)$ indicates that DS u_1 owns digital content $cont$. $send(u_2, u_3, cont)$ corresponds to an action where u_2 propagates digital content $cont$ to u_3.

Domain Policy Creation. Domain policies are created using meta-domain policies from the meta-domain or other domains. Algorithm 1 shows the procedure for a domain that creates domain policies whose meta domain is e_m.

An array, $pols^{(d)}$, is initially created by calling a utility function, `new_array()`, for storing a list of policies (step 1). e_m's meta-domain policies are stored in a list of policies $pols^{(m)}$ by calling `getMetaDomainPolicies(`e_m`)` that return the meta-policies obtained from a database in this domain or retrieve them from e_m (step 2). The appropriateness of all meta-domain policies in schema and content is examined (step 3). Function `verify(`p_i`)` examines whether policies are valid comparing them with meta-policies such as the ones from the root domain if they can be obtained (step 4). If a policy is verified, it is instantiated by calling function `instantiate(·)` as a new policy encoding abstract axioms in concrete data types and action types used in this domain (step 5), and it is registered in the policy list (step 6). For example, an instantiated policy applying the above approach to policy P0.a is

$$(P1) : \neg doable(a) \Leftarrow subject(u_1) \wedge subject(u_2) \wedge own(u_1, data)$$
$$\wedge\ action(send(u_1, u_2, data), a) \wedge \neg consent(u_1, a)$$
$$\wedge\ data\_type(data, medical\_records).$$

In policy P1, axiom $data\_type(\cdot)$ is added to constrain the specified data type of personal data. Here, the administrator of this domain restricts the propagation of personal medical records without obtaining the DS's consent strengthening the meta-domain policies as baseline policies.

Next, the administrator of this domain creates a list of domain specific policies $pols$ by calling function `createDomainSpecificPolicies(·)` (step 9). Each policy created in the above step is verified (step 11) and its relationship with existing policies is checked. The relationships between two policies are listed in Fig. 3 [13].

Algorithm 1. createDomainPolicies(e_m)

1: $pols^{(d)} \leftarrow$ new_array()
2: $pols^{(m)} \leftarrow$ getMetaDomainPolicies(e_m)
3: **for all** i such that $p_i \in pols^{(m)}$ **do**
4:    **if** verify(p_i) = true, **then**
5:        $p_i \leftarrow$ instantiate(p_i)
6:        $pols^{(d)}.add(p_i)$
7:    **end if**
8: **end for**
9: $pols \leftarrow$ createDomainSpecificPolicies()
10: **for all** j such that $p_j \in pols$ **do**
11:    **if** verify(p_j) = true, **then**
12:        **for all** k such that $p_k \in pols^{(d)}$ **do**
13:            **if** $p_k.diverges(p_j)$, **then**
14:                $pols^{(d)}.del(p_k)$
15:            **else if** $p_k.extends(p_j)$, **then**
16:                $pols^{(d)}.del(p_k)$
17:                $pols^{(d)}.add(p_j)$
18:            **else if** $p_k.shuffles(p_j)$, **then**
19:                $p \leftarrow$ createMeetPolicy(p_k, p_j)
20:                $pols^{(d)}.del(p_k)$
21:                $pols^{(d)}.add(p)$
22:            **end if**
23:        **end for**
24:    **end if**
25: **end for**
26: **return** $pols^{(d)}$

Policy Similarity Type	Authorized Requests
p_i Converges p_j	$p_i = p_j$
p_i Diverges p_j	p_i p_j
p_i Restricts p_j	p_i p_j
p_i Extends p_j	p_i p_j
p_i Shuffles p_j	p_i p_j

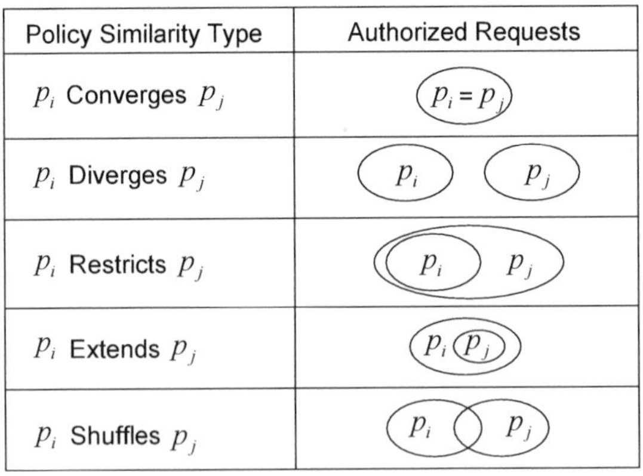

Fig. 3. Similarity Types of Policies

There are five types of similarity in policies, "converges", "diverges", "restricts", "extends", and "shuffles". Note that the similarity between two policies is viewed with respect to which of their conditions hold and that the area covered by a circle representing a policy corresponds to the scope with which it grants execution. Of these, the relationship between an existing policy instantiated from a meta-policy and a new policy created as being domain specific one corresponds to "diverges" (step 13); the existing policy is registered (step 14), since the policy has a different constraint from that of the existing one. If the relationship corresponds to "extends" (step 15), the existing policy is deleted and the new policy is registered (steps 16–17). Otherwise, if the two policies are in a "shuffles" relationship (step 18), a policy for the union of the existing and the new one is newly created by calling function `createMeetPolicy(·)` (step 19); the existing one is deleted (step 20), and the new intersection policy is added into the list of domain policies (step 21). Finally, this function returns a set of registered domain policies (step 26). Note that the above approach to integrating policies strengthens policy constraints except for "converges" and "restricts" cases in which the existing policy encompasses the new one.

Subject Policy Creation. Subject policies in a domain are policies for a particular DS restricting a specific type of the DS's personal data within a certain context.

If the data are created by the domain by which they are managed or if the DS owns the data and delegates their management to the domain, the subject policies are created using the domain policies. The domain policies are instantiated for the DS in the same way as described by Algorithm 1. For example, policy P2 has an application for the same approach and modus ponens to policy P1.

$$(P2) : \neg doable(a) \Leftarrow subject(Alice) \wedge subject(Bob) \wedge own(Alice, data)$$
$$\wedge \ action(send(Alice, Bob, data), a) \wedge \neg consent(Alice, a)$$
$$\wedge \ data\_type(data, medical\_records).$$

In contrast, if the data originally propagate from a different domain acting as a DC to a domain acting as a DP, the agreed upon policies are provided by the DC as a result of the policy being adjusted between the two domains. Here, the DP domain incorporates the agreed upon policies into their subject policies to handle the data. The detailed on the procedure are explained in the following section.

4.2   Policy Agreement between Administrative Domains

Algorithm 2 has the procedure for DP entity e_p requesting and obtaining DS u's personal data whose attribute type is at from DC entity e_c.

DP e_p initially retrieves the subject policies for DC e_c (controller policies) by calling `getControllorPolicies(·)` (step 1). e_p obtains its subject policies (processor policies) for data type at and DS u by calling `getProcessorPolicies(·)`

Algorithm 2. getDataWithPolicies(at, u, e_p, e_c)

1: $pols^{(c)} \leftarrow$ getControllorPolicies(at, u, e_p, e_c)
2: $pols^{(p)} \leftarrow$ getProcessorPolicies(at, u)
3: **for all** j such that $p_j \in pols^{(p)}$ **do**
4:     **if** $\neg(\exists p \in pols^{(c)})$; $p.converges(p_j)$ or $p.extends(p_j)$, **then**
5:         **return** $null$
6:     **end if**
7: **end for**
8: $pols^{(a)} \leftarrow$ getAgreedPolicies$(at, u, pols^{(p)}, e_p, e_c)$
9: **for all** k such that $p_k \in pols^{(a)}$ **do**
10:     **if** verify$(p_k) =$ false or $\neg(\exists q \in pols^{(p)})$; $q.converges(p_k)$, **then**
11:         **return** $null$
12:     **end if**
13: **end for**
14: save$(pols^{(a)})$
15: $hash\_val \leftarrow$ HMAC$_K(pols^{(a)}.id \parallel e_p)$
16: $data \leftarrow$ getData$(at, u, e_p, e_c, hash\_val)$
17: **return** $data$

(step 2). Every policy contained in $pols^{(p)}$ is checked whether it has a "converges" or "extends" relationship with a policy contained in $pols^{(c)}$ or not, since e_p needs to comply with the controller policies that e_c presents (steps 3–7). If no processor policy satisfies a controller policy, this function returns null and e_p cannot obtain the requested data since e_p and e_c cannot agree on how data are handled.

If the processor policies are appropriate, e_p sends a request to e_c for policy agreement on handling the specified data invoking getAgreedPolicies$(\cdot)$ and obtains agreed upon policies $pols^{(a)}$ (step 8). e_p verifies the agreed upon policies and checks whether all policies contained in $pols^{(a)}$ are the same as policies $pols^{(p)}$ or not (steps 9–13). If the agreed upon policies are appropriate, e_p stores them to confirm the contract on the personal information practices between e_p and e_c (step 14).

The procedure for data retrieval is executed in steps 15–16. A keyed hashing for message authentication code (HMAC) [16] mechanism is used to access the data. HMAC$_K(\cdot)$ indicates a HMAC function returning a hash value. Operator "$\parallel$" stands for a concatenation of two strings. Here, the strings of the identifier of agreed upon policies $pols^{(a)}$ and e_p are concatenated and given as input to the above function (step 15). This hash value, as well as at, u, e_p, and e_c, is required as a credential to call function getData$(\cdot)$, in which e_p sends a request to e_c for u's data at and obtains the specified data from e_c (steps 16–17).

This credential-issuing scheme based on agreement enables fine-grained control of access, since the credential required for data cannot be obtained until its requestor has agreed on data practices.

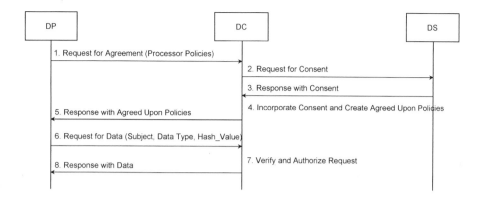

Fig. 4. Data Controller's Policy and Procedure for Data Provisioning

4.3 Control of Data Access and Incorporation of Subject Preferences

A domain's subject policies are generally not sufficient to enforce them when the domain attempts to make a decision to authorize a data access request because it is difficult for a domain's administrators to statically specify any constraints dependent on data types and DSs, or because it is impossible for a DS to specify his or her subject preferences unless conditions are presented. If the policies include a DS's decision or consent, the domain especially needs to interact with the DS and obtain it at runtime. Since this DS's decision or consent indicates one of the DS's subject preferences, they need to be incorporated into a domain's subject policies.

Figure 4 outlines the procedure when a DC receives requests from a DP in accordance with Algorithm 2. The procedure includes a DC's control to access managed personal data and dynamically incorporate the subject preferences of the DS.

When the DP sends a request for attaching an agreement to its processor policies (step 1), the DC verifies the request message and checks with its controller policies, and requests for a consent to the DS that owns the target data to consent by describing how the data will be used by the DP (step 2). The DS shows the consent to the DC, which is one of the subject preferences. Therefore, the consent is incorporated into controller policies and agreed upon policies are created based on the updated controller policies (step 4). The policies are agreements including an identifier that can be used to identify the authenticity of the data request arriving from the DP. After the DC responds with the above agreed upon policies (step 5), the DP makes a new request for the DS's personal data with a hash value (step 6). This value is verified to authenticate the received request from the DP, reproducing a value with the received identifiers. The use of HMAC protects the resource from snooping and extension attacks (step 7). Finally, the requested data are propagated to the DP (step 8).

In the above example, a DC incorporates a DS's consent into its subject policies at runtime when a decision on access control to propagate data is needed. In the same way, a DP also incorporates a DS's consent to process the DS's data at runtime when the DP attempts to do so.

4.4   Protection from Unauthorized Policy Updates

DC needs to have an access control mechanism for unauthorized policy updates and modifications. Here, the subject policies of DCs are regarded as restricted resources in the same way as personal data at DC.

Whenever a DC deploys new policies such as agreed upon policies and domain policies, it verifies their validity and authenticity. If the DC finds any inappropriateness in policies, it stops integrating them to mitigate the risk of unfair information practices.

5   Discussion

This section discusses several topics and issues related to the proposed model and framework.

5.1   Retaining Data Management

Policies in the proposed model that reflect local laws or regulations of social organizations or computer systems are appropriately provided beyond administrative domains in distributed environments since the model has a hierarchical structure for creating and propagating policies and supports a policy propagation chain in accordance with data propagation. By means of this approach, the administrator of a root domain can retain the management of data enforcing their provisioned policies that reflect his or her intentions regarding data governance even after the data have been propagated in the distributed system. In addition, participating parties in the system can clarify their liabilities concerning data practices and improve the accountability of their activities on handling data. To further support the lifecycle management of data and policies, a mechanism for updating provisioned policies at runtime is needed if it is difficult for an administrator to statically specify policies containing various types of constraints.

5.2   Policy Conflicts

The proposed model facilitates the avoidance of policy conflicts between entities detecting similarities between policies when new policies are created or integrated. Since DP entities need to accept DC's controlling policies or strengthen their constraints, there is no room for policy negotiation in policy between them. This is appropriate from the governance and compliance viewpoints of a root domain's administrator. However, this approach may reduce the expressiveness of policies when flexible representations such as exceptional action rules are needed.

Although this is a problem involving a trade-off, finding an appropriate balance between administrative restrictive descriptions and rich representations of policies is an open issue that needs further investigation.

5.3 Directive and Recommendation Policies

As explained in Section 4.1, governance policies state that personal information can be managed by DS as its owner from a user-centric perspective. However, it is difficult for a DS to take an appropriate action in all environments. For example, privacy laws and privacy guidelines such as those of the OECD [17] dictate that enterprises should take into account the consent given by people to use their data for specified purposes. However, people may possibly act inappropriately if they do not understand what their consent involves, which unfortunately does not match the intentions of legislators of privacy-related guidelines. In such cases, administrators can specify complementary directive policies stating that enterprises should provide sufficient explanations to people about how their data are used or that enterprises should suggest to them possible actions that can be taken.

6 Conclusion and Future Work

This paper described a policy provisioning model in which distinct entities in distributed environments collaboratively create and propagate data handling policies. Algorithms for creating and integrating policies enable data handling policies to be deployed and enforced to securely and privacy control access to personal data in an enhancing manner. The proposed framework helps to manage the lifecycle of personal data using their handling policies that reflect the intentions of the system administrator and their owner. Future work includes that on updating policies and resolving conflicts in them.

References

1. Byun, J.W., Bertino, E., Li, N.: Purpose Based Access Control of Complex Data for Privacy Protection. In: Proceedings of the 10th ACM Symposium on Access Control Models and Technologies (SACMAT 2005), pp. 102–110 (2005)
2. Ardagna, C.A., Cremonini, M., De Capitani di Vimercati, S., Samarati, P.: A Privacy-Aware Access Control System. Journal of Computer Security 16(4), 369–397 (2008)
3. Gomi, H.: A Persistent Data Tracking Mechanism for User-Centric Identity Governance. Identity in the Information Society (March 2010), doi:10.1007/s12394-010-0069-4
4. Schneck, P.: Persistent Access Control to Prevent Piracy of Digital Information. Proceedings of the IEEE 87(7), 1239–1250 (1999)
5. Sibert, O., Bernstein, D., Wie, D.: DigiBox: A Self-Protecting Container for Information Commerce. In: Proceedings of the 1st Conference on USENIX Workshop on Electronic Commerce (WOEC 1995), p. 15 (1995)

6. Karjoth, G., Schunter, M., Waidner, M.: Platform for Enterprise Privacy Practices: Privacy-Enabled Management of Customer Data. In: Dingledine, R., Syverson, P.F. (eds.) PET 2002. LNCS, vol. 2482, pp. 69–84. Springer, Heidelberg (2003)
7. Casassa Mont, M., Pearson, S., Bramhall, P.: Towards Accountable Management of Identity Privacy: Sticky Policies and Enforceable Tracing Services. In: Mařík, V., Štěpánková, O., Retschitzegger, W. (eds.) DEXA 2003. LNCS, vol. 2736, pp. 377–382. Springer, Heidelberg (2003)
8. Liberty Alliance Project: Liberty IGF Privacy Constraints Specification (2008), http://www.projectliberty.org/specs
9. W3C: The Platform for Privacy Preferences 1.0 (P3P1.0) Specification (2002), http://www.w3.org/TR/P3P/
10. W3C: A P3P Preference Exchange Language 1.0 (APPEL1.0) (2002), http://www.w3.org/TR/P3P-preferences/
11. OASIS: eXtensible Access Control Markup Language, XACML (2005)
12. IBM: Enterprise Privacy Authorization Language (EPAL 1.2) (2003), http://www.w3.org/Submission/2003/SUBM-EPAL-20031110/
13. Mazzoleni, P., Crispo, B., Sivasubramanian, S., Bertino, E.: XACML Policy Integration Algorithms. ACM Transactions on Information and System Securiry 11(1), 1–29 (2008)
14. Belokosztolszki, A., Moody, K.: Meta-Policies for Distributed Role-Based Access Control Systems. In: Proceedings of the Third International Workshop on Policies for Distributed Systems and Networks (POLICY 2002), pp. 3–18 (2002)
15. Bettini, C., Jajodia, S., Sean Wang, X., Wijesekera, D.: Provisions and Obligations in Policy Management and Security Applications. In: Proceedings of the 28th International Conference on Very Large Data Bases (VLDB 2002), pp. 502–513 (2002)
16. Krawczyk, H., Bellare, M., Canetti, R.: HMAC: Keyed-Hashing for Message Authentication, RFC 2104 (1997)
17. OECD: OECD Guidelines on the Protection of Privacy and Transborder Flows of Personal Data (2004), http://www.oecd.org/document/18/0,2340,en_2649_201185_1815186_1_1_1_1,00.html

Author Index